The Mourning Voice

Cornell Studies in Classical Philology

EDITED BY

Frederick M. Ahl, Kevin Clinton, John E. Coleman,

Gail Fine, Judith R. Ginsburg, Terence Irwin, G. M. Kirkwood, David Mankin,

Gordon M. Messing, Alan J. Nussbaum, Hayden Pelliccia, Pietro Pucci,

Jeffrey S. Rusten, Danuta Shanzer, Barry S. Strauss

VOLUME LVIII

The Mourning Voice:
An Essay on Greek Tragedy
by *Nicole Loraux*

ALSO IN THE TOWNSEND LECTURES

The Mourning Voice

An Essay on Greek Tragedy

Nicole Loraux

TRANSLATED FROM THE FRENCH BY

Elizabeth Trapnell Rawlings

Foreword by Pietro Pucci

Cornell University Press

Ithaca and London

First published 2002 by Cornell University Press

Printed in the United States of America

Library of Congress Cataloging-in-Publication Data

Loraux, Nicole.
　[Voix endeuillée. English]
　The mourning voice : an essay on Greek tragedy / by Nicole Loraux ;
translated from the French by Elizabeth Trapnell Rawlings ; foreword by
Pietro Pucci.
　　p. cm.—(Cornell studies in classical philology ; v. 58. The
Townsend lectures)
　　Includes bibliographical references and index.
　　ISBN 0-8014-3830-6 (cloth : alk. paper)
　　1. Greek drama (Tragedy)—History and criticism.　2.
Greece—Civilization—To 146 B.C.　3. Grief in literature.　I. Title.
II. Cornell studies in classical philology ; v. 58.　III. Cornell studies
in classical philology. Townsend lectures.
　PA3131 .L6713 2002
　882'.0109—dc21　　　　　　　　　　2001006629

Cornell University Press strives to use environmentally responsible
suppliers and materials to the fullest extent possible in the publishing
of its books. Such materials include vegetable-based, low-VOC inks
and acid-free papers that are recycled, totally chlorine-free, or partly
composed of nonwood fibers. For further information, visit our
website at www.cornellpress.cornell.edu.

Cloth printing　　10 9 8 7 6 5 4 3 2 1

For Pietro Pucci, for Gregory Nagy

In this hell-sepulcher what did they do?
What can be done in a sepulcher? They died.
What can be done in a hell? They sang. For where
There is no more hope, song remains.

> Victor Hugo, *Les Misérables*, Part Four: Saint-Denis
> and the Idyll of the rue Plumet

CONTENTS

Contents

FOREWORD

In the spring of 1993 Nicole Loraux delivered the annual Townsend Lectures at Cornell University. The title of her lecture series was "The Voice of Mourning in Attic Tragedy." In 1999 Gallimard published the French version of these lectures under the title *La voix endeuillée. Essai sur la tragédie grecque,* and it is the text of the French book, with some emendations conforming to the original typescript of the lectures, that now appears in English translation by Elizabeth Trapnell Rawlings.

Loraux's appeal to a renewed Nietzschean reading of Greek tragedy appeared then, as it appears now, as a polemical manifesto against some of the main tendencies of criticism. She emphasizes the paramount importance of the chorus, of the music, of the *phonē* at the expense of the *logos,* and of the political, ethical, and religious contexts, a direction that certainly challenges a large part of contemporary criticism. One need only read essays of the 1990s, often published as collective works, to find an almost unilateral chorus of voices insisting on "the communitarian character of the Athenian scene," on the expectation of the *polis* and of the theatrical audience for works that "consolidate the social identity and maintain the cohesion of the community" (O. Longo in the programmatic piece opening Froma Zeitlin and John Winkler's collection of essays *Nothing to Do with Dionysus?: Athenian Drama in Its Social Context* [Princeton University Press, 1990, pp. 13–14]). In the opening pages of the collection titled *Theater and Society in the Classical World* (University of Michigan Press, 1993), the editor, Ruth Scodel, emphasizes the power of dramatic rituals to achieve "social integration" (p. 2). Analogously, in *History, Tragedy, Theory: Dialogues on Athenian Drama* (University of Texas Press, 1995), edited by Barbara Goff, and in *The Cambridge Companion to Greek Tragedy* (Cambridge University Press, 1997), edited by P. E. Easterling, many essays take a decidedly historical slant. Paul Cartledge, in the first pages of the *Cambridge Companion,* proclaims that "tragedy . . . was itself an active ingredient and a major one of political foreground, featuring in the everyday consciousness and even in the nocturnal dreams of Athenians."

It would be wrong to assert that most of these contributors are unaware of the critical distance that tragedy often takes from the conventional ideology. Many of the authors in the cited collections, and in particular Scodel, Goff, and Cartledge (p. 21) in their opening essays, underline this point. Yet it is fair to say that the main emphasis falls on the idea that the political and religious content of tragedy constitutes its essential meaning and that this content essentially upholds the ideology of the *polis.*

This presentation, though short and schematic, allows the reader to measure the extraordinary novelty and the polemical punch of Loraux's book. For she reinterprets and revises the stance and the importance of these sociological and political claims and considers tragedy essentially as a ceaseless song of lamentation, more specifically a song of mourning lament (*thrēnos*). She emphasizes the articulate and inarticulate utterances of the voice (*phonē*) at the expense of the *logos,* of the lyric at the expense of the spoken drama; she illuminates the power of the music, of the flute, an instrument that is foreign to the Greek civic world, and harks back to the Nietzschean conflict and harmony that divide and unite Dionysus and Apollo.

As one can see from this description, Loraux's assessment of tragedy is not a new version of the thesis that posits tragedy as a producer of affects and emotions in the style of William B. Stanford (*Greek Tragedy and the Emotions: An Introductory Study* [Routledge, 1983]) or Malcolm Heath (*The Poetics of Greek Tragedy* [Stanford University Press, 1987]), but a new evaluation of the role that lament, voice, and music play in the civic space. For indeed within the ethical and political walls of the *polis,* the overly emotional lament for the dead gets a very bad reception: mourning, especially that of women, is banished by the laws of the city, and the memory of the dead is limited to the chastened and controlled form of the official funeral orations. Tragedy therefore imposes itself in the Athenian political context as an "antipolitical" representation, and to some extent even as foreign. Phrynichus's play *The Capture of Miletus* brought the audience to tears and led to the proscription of contemporary historical events as themes for tragedy.

Loraux begins by directly facing the challenge of difficult questions: She analyzes how Sartre gave Euripides' *Trojan Women* a political thrust and how, in order to do so, he had to purify it of its musical "oratorio"-like character. She argues successfully, marshaling a wealth of evidence and subtle interpretation, against the "political" significance that some critics attribute both to the ceremonies that were staged in the theater before the beginning of the theatrical performances, and to the gatherings that were held for exceptional occasions in the space of the theater.

I believe that she is also right in questioning the paramount political significance that some critics accord to *The Persians*. Many of its spectators at the initial performance were the warriors who eight years earlier had defeated the Persians and caused the horrible losses that Xerxes laments in the play; they were nevertheless forced to feel pity for the enemy they defeated. Xerxes himself, however, prompts the audience also to feel pride and pleasure at the performance of his lament when he defines the defeat as *lupra, kharmata d'ekhthrois,* "grievous for us, but a joy for the enemy"(1034). This wink to the audience is quick, almost sandwiched between utterances of overwhelming pathos, but undeniable. We touch here a particularly jarring oxymoron of emotions without any resolution. Perhaps we may understand it if we recall the famous simile of *Odyssey* VIII, 521–531, where Odysseus, after having listened to Demodocus sing about Odysseus's and the other Achaean heroes' capture of Troy, weeps just like a Trojan hero's widow, desperately crying over the body of her husband while she is being beaten and dragged away into slavery. There the *Odyssey* sets up an identity between the pain of the victor and that of the vanquished. Through the performance of *The Persians,* before an audience of *andres* (warriors), tragedy universalizes them, decontextualizes them from their position as citizens of the victorious city, and turns them into human beings who feel like *anthrōpoi,* like mortal men, and are therefore able both to feel joy for their triumph and to recognize their fraternity in death with their enemies.

In the course of these arguments, Loraux defines the two meanings that she attaches to the "antipolitical" label: first, it designates positions and stances that go beyond politics, and second, it indicates practices and representations that are consciously or unconsciously opposed or foreign to the ideology of the polis. Of course a neat distinction between these two connotations is not easy to draw. The difficult question that arises here (of which Loraux is perfectly conscious) is to what extent the "representation" as such, by producing an effect of distanciation and of estrangement (a special language and style, fictional features, and the like), renders politically ineffective, or neutral, that which, if practiced off the stage, would be politically scandalous and unacceptable. This effect is undeniable, but how and at what level it operates is difficult to say. It is easy, on the contrary, to realize that the censure of all political regimes proves that this artistic effect of distanciation is not felt and appreciated by the political powers.

Any new interpretation that, like this one, unsettles received opinions on a text always uncovers new linguistic features and elaborates them in a new way. The central chapters of the book bring to our eyes and ears the sounds and the utterances of the mourning lamentations that constitute the core of so many tragedies. The reader will learn (in the course of some superb analyses of Sophocles' *Electra* and Euripides' *Trojan Women*) about the opposition between the civic and the tragic meanings of *aei,* "always," the tragic referring to the ceaseless performance of the lamentation, while the civic *aei* constantly proposes renewals and confidence. Furthermore, this *aei* or *aiei* enters into a phonetic and sympathetic interrelation with *aiai,* the scream of pain, and other similar utterances—*aiazein, ia*—that the tragic voice makes resonate even in the name of Aiax (*Aias*). We hear the sound of the tragic *thrēnos* ("mourning lament"), we are told about the troubling sound of the flute (*aulos*), about the difference between the *goos* (lament) and the *thrēnos,* a difference that some critics consider fully erased in tragedy.

It is in connection with this musical and disturbing character of tragedy that Loraux recalls *The Birth of Tragedy*, and produces a rereading of Nietzsche's thesis. She begins by analyzing the Bacchic and Apollonian utterances, the cries of *iakkhē, euoi,* and the intriguing presence of the Apollonian *paean* in tragedy, and deepens the distance, even the incompatibility, between the Apollonian language/music (the rejection of Hades and lamentations) and the tragic Dionysian music and utterances. Apollo, however, is more than present in tragedy, especially in Euripides' plays. The incompatibility is at the same time contiguity, and Loraux illustrates this contiguity in a masterly analysis of the Apollonian and Dionysian features that intermingle in *The Choephoroi* and *The Trojan Women*. The oxymoron is again the figure that marks tragedy.

One is reminded of many Euripidean tragedies in which the Dionysian and Apollonian features intersect. I think, for instance, of the *Orestes,* where Orestes' madness, caused by his obedience to Apollo, is described through Dionysian images (e.g., 35ff., 316 ff., 834–835). At the end of the play even Pylades, the man of Delphi, the one who in Aeschylus reminded Orestes of his duty toward Apollo, is described, together with Orestes, as a "thyrsus-less baccant"(1490).

The critical wealth of Loraux's insights does not need emphasis. Loraux could have used the conventional arguments that critics parade when they want to suggest Euripides' antipolitical views (his criticism of the traditional gods, his nihilism) or to illustrate Sophocles' analogous stance (the hidden, unreadable figures of his gods), and so on. But she has developed her own original antipolitical perceptions in a new portrait of tragedy.

She mentions once the "joy" (*ekharēn*) that Dionysus claims (in Aristophanes' *Frogs,* 1028–1029) to have felt in hearing Darius's lament in Aeschylus's *Persians*; this feeling of joy, experienced by the god of tragedy, proves that even in the play that theorizes the didactic effect of tragedy, tragedy prompts reactions that fall completely outside the conceptual field of "instruction." Tragedy gives pleasure. Of course Loraux could have mentioned all the expressions that the archaic Greeks used, before Plato, to define the effects poetry produced on them; these terms evoke feelings of joy, sweetness, charm, pathos, deception, fear, and others. No political pride, no educational edification. (See G. Lanata, *Poetica preplatonica* [Florence, 1963], and Heath, *The Poetics of Greek Tragedy*).

Loraux's book invites the reader to continue her exploration in the conflicting and yet intermingling features of Greek tragedy, of the lyrical and dramatic parts, of the bemoaning utterances and the *logoi,* of the political and the antipolitical stances, of Apollonian and Dionysian utterances. For it is conflict that, according to Heraclitus, produces harmony. Even the *katharsis* (the purgation of the emotions) is implicated in the power-play of this concordant and discordant structure, and therefore pivots between the effect of purgation and consolation and the insatiability of grief. For this grief is inalienable: it grasps and defines human beings not as citizens of a political community but as mortal men and women.

PIETRO PUCCI

TRANSLATOR'S NOTE

Unless otherwise noted, quotations from ancient Greek sources—identified by line number—are direct translations from Nicole Loraux's own reading of the Greek texts.

The quotation from Victor Hugo's *Les Misérables* in the dedication is from the translation of Lee Fahnestock and Norman MacAfee (Penguin Books, 1987), Part 4, book VII, chapter 2, p. 992. Quotations from Nietzsche are from Walter Kaufmann's translation of *The Birth of Tragedy and the Case of Wagner* (Random House, 1967).

The translator thanks Pietro Pucci for suggesting certain alterations to the French-language edition to make the text conform to the original French transcript of the Townsend Lectures.

[I]

GREEK TRAGEDY: POLITICAL DRAMA OR ORATORIO?

In which the contemporary reader rediscovers the significance of oratorio in Greek tragedy.

"Yes, congratulate them, those who started this war!"
CASSANDRA, in Euripides, *The Trojan Women* (382)

"Surely it is the duty of the wise man to prevent war."
CASSANDRA, in *The Trojan Women* (399)

La femme comme source du mal, de la guerre de Troie, etc.
[Woman as the root of all evil, the Trojan War, etc.]
NIETZSCHE, *La naissance de la tragédie* (fragments posthumes)

And here the sublime and celebrated art of Attic tragedy and the dramatic dithyramb presents itself as the common goal of both these tendencies whose mysterious union, after many and long precursory struggles, found glorious consummation in this child—at once Antigone and Cassandra.
NIETZSCHE, *The Birth of Tragedy*

On March 10, 1965, Jean-Paul Sartre's adaptation of Euripides' *Trojan Women* was performed by the Théâtre Nationale Populaire, under the direction of Georges Wilson. While this may appear to be an indirect starting point for a work devoted to the mourning voice of tragedy—or rather, the mourning voice within and, as it were, "beneath" tragedy, as if mourning were one of the principal subtexts in a tragic text—I have chosen it not simply because I wish to establish a thoroughly French frame of reference from the very beginning. I also want to begin this study of tragedy by setting it within the context of the reception of the tragic genre. Hence my approach will be to look at tragedy not only as a text, but also and above all as theater, taking into account the effect produced on a particular public.

The public in question here is of course the *theatron,*[1] that characteristically Athenian gathering of citizens brought together for the solemn celebration of the Great Dionysia. At a certain point, then, we shall have to inquire into the scope, collective or individual, of the tragic effect, while keeping in mind that any answer will always look a great deal like a pure construct. Because we approach ancient tragedy from the point of view of our own time, with its own problematic, we shall also be concerned with the effect produced on the contemporary audience we represent today, and specifically on Sartre's very different audience in 1965. We shall thus proceed by moving back and forth among three focal points: the tragic texts both studied as texts and restored to their historical context; the present-day reception of tragedy; and the reception of tragedy in ancient times, which I shall attempt to reconstruct—or invent—beginning from texts whose own reception is thought to be implicit.

I must point out that this movement back and forth between the present and the past is also rooted in personal experience: the practice of translating Greek tragedy for theater. The translator is caught between the categorical imperative of fidelity to the ancient text and the transposition necessary to enable a modern public to understand something of what the fifth-century Athenian audience heard in a performance of tragedy. If the objective is to raise contemporary spectators to the level needed to understand Aeschylus's *Oresteia* or Euripides' *Hecuba* or *The Trojan Women,* and not to bring Aeschylus or Euripides down to the level of a modern audience, which is out of the question, how should the translator proceed? This very practical question becomes especially important when the translator is, by profession, a reader of Greek tragic texts, little inclined to make concessions to contemporary taste. My experience as both translator and scholar has no doubt influenced the approach I shall adopt here.

But it is time to return to Sartre—since it was he who provided the basis for this presentation—and to his 1965 adaptation of *The Trojan Women.*

Sartre had not written for the theater since 1960, when *The Condemned of Altona* appeared, so *The Trojan Women* was a way for him to reconnect with the stage. Why, then, did he choose to adapt an existing play in 1965 rather than write in his own name, and why did he adapt a Greek tragedy?

Sartre replies to this question in an interview with the writer Bernard Pingaud, which serves as an introduction to the published text.[2] From a strictly descriptive point of view, there is nothing to add to Sartre's remarks, for he formulated with perfect clarity what he meant to do and what he in fact did. Before reading his introduction, however, I began by reading Euripides' text alongside Sartre's adaptation. This reading, prompted entirely by my twofold interest in tragedy as quite specifically Greek, and in its most contemporary representations, revealed that Sartre's adaptation provides us with a Sartrian interpretation of Euripides' text. This is hardly surprising: any writer attempts to put his own mark on a production, even one destined to be brief.

Sartre's *Trojan Women*

A close look at Euripides' *Trojan Women* and at the adaptation leaves little doubt that the destructive fury of the Greeks is emphasized in Sartre's version. Athena's fury, in the prologue, prefigures that of the Greeks: Athena, even though she has turned against her former protégés, is thought to express something like the very essence of the Greek will for evil.[3] All the action proceeds from this premise. Thus daylight, which is just breaking over the Greek tragedy (when the drama begins, Hecuba says "my suffering before dawn, daughter, has sent me here" [*TW* 182–183]), yields, in the adaptation, to a profound night, the evocation of a "black sky" (*TW-S*, v), and a celebration of the breaking dawn, "horribly beautiful" (*TW-S*, ix).[4] Similarly, wherever possible Sartre inserts deaths or corpses and fire, omnipresent as "flames and black flakes," "smoking, blackening stones," "living torches," anticipating the final conflagration of the city, although that is only briefly mentioned in Sartre's version. All of this is obviously fraught with pathos, which is precisely what Sartre intended.

Was tragedy not bleak enough for the use Sartre wished to make of it? Such a sentiment seems to be what dictated the modifications—additions or omissions—Sartre made to Euripides' plot. One example will demonstrate: "The duty of a wise man is indeed to avoid war," concludes Cassandra (*TW* 400), after explaining at length why she rejoices in her union with Agamemnon, knowing that she will cause his downfall. Sartre not only has no need for this observation and erases it from

his text, he comments on the omission and assigns it exemplary significance:

> That "the duty of a wise man is indeed to avoid war," as Cassandra
> says, goes without saying: the condition of one and all is proof
> enough; I preferred to give Poseidon the last word: "It'll kill all of
> you." (Sartre, "Introduction")

If we are to understand Cassandra's remark as something more than a
truism, we will have to invest it with the precise meaning appropriate in
Euripides' Greece—and evoke, for example, a number of statements
scattered here and there about war as natural; only then can we evaluate
the real significance of Cassandra's contested statement.[5] Clearly, such
was not Sartre's intention. Nevertheless, there is a great deal to be said
about Poseidon's reappearance at the end of the play—Sartre's invention—to carry the message of his *Trojan Women*. In Euripides' tragedy,
the spectator must interpret what he sees when the Trojan women
slowly make their way to the ships of their Greek masters while the city
behind them burns; in contrast, Sartre has Poseidon[6] address a passive
spectator, or possibly one looking for political and intellectual guidance.
To a spectator so inclined, Sartre is speaking of contemporary war, in
this case, of the United States' total involvement in the Vietnam War.

However, I must point out another type of intervention in the text:
Sartre's introduction of psychology into the play. Perhaps this should
not be surprising. After all, *Imagination: A Psychological Critique*,[7] published in 1940, was one of Sartre's early works. Nevertheless, the psychological approach clearly disfigures the most authentically tragic quality of *The Trojan Women*, a quality that, by contrast, can come through
brilliantly, as it did in Jean-Pierre Vincent's 1998 production of Euripides' *play*.

The same is true of the stage directions systematically inserted in the
text, in which Sartre comments on the reactions and emotions of the
characters in order to direct acting and staging. For example, in scene ii,
Poseidon, standing before Athena, "turns, sees her and angrily goes to
leave;" in scene iii the stage directions indicate that Hecuba's "courage
failed her. She stopped thinking clearly"; and another stage direction, at
the beginning of scene vii, indicates rather labored staging: "Hecuba
now looks coldly at Andromache and sees Astyanax" (*TW-S*, vii).
Again, I am not pleading for a historically accurate reconstitution of the
tragic genre, which, at least during its most prolific golden age, gave no

stage directions, save for the bare minimum embedded in the text. Sartre's stage directions, however, are conspicuously psychologizing, whereas the rule of coherence of Greek tragedy is that there is nothing to be known about the characters and their feelings other than what is said in the text.

We can find many other indications of this tendency to incorporate psychology in the text of Sartre's *Trojan Women*. For example, Cassandra's madness (*mania*): whereas Euripides insists it is Dionysian (*TW* 170), for Sartre it is simply illness: "she's mad" (scene iii); Euripides' phrase "Your turn to lead the dance, *Evan, evoi*" (*TW* 326) becomes instead an image of "Crazy Cassandra." As for the maenad in lines 348–349, she simply disappears. Finally, the clause "if it were not Apollo who made you crazy" (*TW* 408)—remarkable in its paradoxical dimension because it posits the problem, dear to Nietzsche, of the links between Apollo and Dionysus—yields to Sartre's blatant rationalist transposition ("if she still had her wits"). Through this translation of inspired bacchism into a clinical insanity worthy of nineteenth-century psychiatry, the relationship to the divine is suppressed. Human beings are consequently all the more vulnerable to elemental passions, and Sartre, developing a tension between Hecuba and Andromache that is almost imperceptible in Euripides, transforms a moment of lyric emotion, in which the voices of the two women alternate (*TW* 575–607), into a bitter exchange between a mother-in-law and her daughter-in-law, each eager to fight like the *petites bourgeoises* they have become in Sartre's hands. "I have never liked you, . . . old woman," says Andromache to Hecuba, who returns the sentiment (*TW-S*, vii).

In short, in the adaptation of *The Trojan Women*, Sartre's theatrical universe has usurped that of Euripides, and the text presents no significant departures from Sartre's own plays. It is a question of tone, of course, but in this case, tone means a great deal. Whereas in Euripides' play the exalted Cassandra grants "their greatest glory" (*TW* 386) to the Trojans for having defended their fatherland to the death, in Sartre's play she says simply:

> We . . . have lost [the war]
> but I am not ashamed.
>   (sc. v)

Indeed, glory is vain, and all that matters is the hatred of the conquered for the conqueror, but from one version to the other, from the evocation of "beautiful death" to the acknowledgment of defeat, the difference for a Greek was more than a nuance. In fact, more than once Sartre's tone replaces a noble style with deliberately banal—if not vulgar—language, but, as we know, existentialism expects a lot from a certain degree of vulgarity. In Euripides' tragedy, after Talthybios has informed Hecuba that Odysseus will be her master, the chorus of women addresses Hecuba and ponders the future for each of them:

> You have learned your fate, my lady.
> What power will decide my own?
> (*TW* 292–293)

In Sartre's text, the question is addressed to Talthybios, who answers it as any servant of the rich and powerful might:

> I know nothing about it.
> It's none of my business.
> They are going to draw lots for the small fry.
> (*TW-S,* iv)

Talthybios displays a certain compunction, in keeping with his role as herald. However, on the side of the powerful, language is a little freer. Here the indignant, wronged husband Menelaus no longer calls Paris "a treacherous guest" (*TW* 864) in a probable allusion to Aeschylus's *pathos* for offended hospitality, but instead refers to "that scum, who was a guest in my palace" (*TW-S,* x).[8] As for women, if they happen to be young, they are obsessed with their own bodies and sexuality. I already mentioned Cassandra, whom the chorus leader urges Hecuba to restrain lest she "jump right into the bed of some Greek" (*TW-S,* v). In Euripides' text, the chorus leader says merely: "My queen, her mind is going, stop her. Her frenzy may lead her to the Greeks' camp"[9] (*TW* 341–342). And there is also Helen, who, with wits (*phrēnes*) deranged by Paris's beauty, becomes a "body damp with desire" (*TW-S,* x).

We are reminded at times, when the tone is less emphatic, of Offenbach's *Belle Hélène;* at least this was my impression as a reader. But Sartre, in his interview with Pingaud, has clearly thought of everything, confirming that the reference was indeed intentional. Actually, I should say multiple references, as the text is packed with quotations from the great works of Western culture, from Pascal to Brecht by way of Mozart and Shakespeare.[10] One might wonder about the purpose of this strategy, but once again the choice was deliberate, even predetermined, and Sartre is so careful to explain his reading of Euripides, in whose hands tragedy "becomes an allusive conversation of clichés," that it is appropriate to cite Beckett and Ionesco "who use the cliché to destroy it from within" (*TW-S*, Introduction, p. 3). But what becomes of the allusive conversation when Sartre adds that "naturally the clearer and bolder the cliché, the more striking the demonstration"? Sartre, in an endless effort to clarify, explains his statement: he claims that the Athenian audience readily understood what would have been meaningless to a French spectator in 1965 if translated word for word, and argues, reasonably, that "If I wish to make this play meaningful, I cannot simply translate it, I must adapt it" (p. 4).

We can all agree that the same contingency is imposed on any contemporary translation of Greek tragedy whenever it is destined for the stage. Still, the categorical imperative of every translator—to faithfully bridge the distance between the original and the translation—demands that the translator/interpreter agree to serve the text rather than use it, unless the avowed intent is to distort it. Without going so far as to characterize Sartre's undertaking as a distortion, I am not certain that his adaptation, justifiable as it is and justified by Sartre himself with regard to the use of clichés, is, always and in every detail, careful to refrain from harmful manipulation.

The question arises concerning a gesture that recurs too often not to be intentional, one that profoundly alters Euripides' tragedy. This is Sartre's systematic transforming into dialogue everything that in Euripides' *Trojan Women* is in the form of discourse (*stasimon*). We find examples in passages of rhetoric such as Cassandra's frequently interrupted harangue in scene vi, expressing her joy at becoming Agamemnon's wife "who will do [the Greeks] more harm" than Helen (*TW-S*, vi), and in the speech Hecuba makes to the chorus after her daughter departs (*TW* 466–510); but it is also the case with moments of lyric emotion, such as the first *stasimon,* which becomes simply dialogue in Sartre's text. Should we view this alteration as necessary to an adaptation like Sartre's in order to make an audience in 1965 (or 2002 for that matter) hear what would have been audible to an Athenian audience, accustomed to the long speeches of the democratic assembly? Is it simply a way of bypassing the dramatic difficulty that the staging of the chorus presents today? Such considerations played a role in the very obvious interventions alluded to above, which were no doubt an attempt to animate, to render more expressive, a text which, by comparison, seems remarkably discreet about its own power.[11]

I believe, however, that Sartre gained another advantage in substituting rapid dialogue for sustained discourse (which demands attentiveness): it gave him an opportunity to orient the listener by inserting commentaries and judgments between the successive stages of an argument. We see an example in scene vii when Hecuba advises Andromache to please her new husband and is rudely interrupted by her daughter-in-law, who says: "Are you, old woman, mother of Hector, giving me a matchmaker's advice? Hah!" (*TW-S,* vii). In Euripides' text, Andromache was content to listen in silence (*TW* 697–704).

Here, in a method that goes from interpretive transposition to interpolation, Sartre modifies *The Trojan Women* from within, and these interventions are of great interest in that they offer a reliable indication of what he expects from Greek tragedy, and of what he rejects in it—and often he rejects what, in my view, are essential elements of the tragic.

Greek Tragedy: Is It Relevant?

Should we conclude that the significance of *The Trojan Women* is strictly political because it was performed during the Great Dionysia of 415 B.C.E., in the same month that the Athenian Assembly voted in favor of the Sicilian expedition? Many commentators think so, seeing in it a condemnation of wars of conquest and, if not a prediction of disaster,[12] then at least a kind of veiled warning. If such was the message, there is nothing to suggest that the Athenians misunderstood it: one could even say, in fact, that they understood its meaning so well that they rejected it, and gave the prize that year to a different tragic author.

It is also possible, however, to propose an entirely different reading of the play, emphasizing that if, of all Euripides's tragedies, *The Trojan Women* is the least dramatic and the one most given to *pathos,* this play is also undeniably the most lyrical.[13] It is particularly interesting to note that not only is there no distinguishing marker in the adaptation of *The Trojan Women* to indicate the lyric passages, which in most translations would be printed in italics; Sartre does not hesitate at times to eliminate them entirely, as if the chorus's complaints annoyed him. For example, in scene xi, Hecuba delivers a long monologue as she bends over the body of Astyanax. Sartre does not hesitate to adopt a strategy that is contrary to his usual method of wagering at every turn on dialogue—and the exception proves the rule since in this case it allows time for the queen's mourning to be transformed into an anticolonialist diatribe; at the same time Sartre erases every trace of the lamentations with which, in the ritual mode of the *kommos,* the women of Troy punctuate Hecuba's threnody and the dressing of the dead child (*TW* 1226–1255).[14] In fact, we must suppose that this rejection was important to Sartre, since he felt the need to justify himself. Yet the explanation remains problematic; we ought therefore to consider it more closely.

It begins with a peremptory affirmation that "this is not a tragedy like *Antigone,* it is an oratorio," and, as if the point were an obvious one, he continues: "I have tried to 'dramatize' it by emphasizing some of the conflicts left implicit in Euripides: the conflict between Andromache and Hecuba,[. . .], Cassandra's erotic fascination, throwing herself into Agamemnon's bed, knowing, however, that she will perish with him" (*TW-S,* Introduction).[15]

Here we understand the reasons for some of the modifications previously observed. Some questions remain, however. Since it appeared necessary to reintroduce drama artificially, why did he choose an "oratorio"? Was the drama that resulted from Sartre's intervention in compliance with the requirements of political theater?

Sartre prepared the answer to these questions as well, an answer that is, as one might expect, both contingent and political. It is shaped by the paradigmatic experience of the French intelligentsia of the time, the Algerian War. Sartre says that he had been "struck" by the success of a performance of Euripides' *Trojan Women* during the Algerian War "with an audience in favor of negotiating with the FLN," because the play was, in his view, "a condemnation of war in general[16] and of colonialist expeditions in particular" (*TW-S,* Introduction); thus, his intention was to reproduce this type of intervention,[17] only this time for the Vietnam War, and with an strongly pro–third–world bias,[18] turning against the West the very Greek culture that it exports as if it were the surest cement of the colonialist ideology.[19]

Thus Sartre's political aim was what led him to a systematic exaggeration of his message. Nothing could be left to chance—in this case to what would be the actual choice between perceptiveness and deafness for the spectator, who was virtually free, as was the Athenian audience, to decipher the tragic ambiguity or not. The most important words of the lesson had to be stressed endlessly, beginning with the Greeks' "barbarity," already denounced by Andromache in Euripides' play in her pathetic cry of rebellion when her son was taken from her to be killed. Helen's grim genealogy—recounted vividly by Andromache in terms that make Helen "an evil demon for so many Greeks and barbarians"

(*TW* 771–772)—disappears from Sartre's text, replaced by a diatribe on torture, on colonial Europe against Africa and Asia, and on the Greeks' groundless boasting of their humanity (*TW-S,* viii). After this, it is logical for Poseidon to return to the stage for a final monologue, to reveal "the tragic dénouement," and acknowledge that "all Cassandra's predictions will come to pass" (*TW-S,* Introduction). This news is comforting from the Trojan point of view, since it implies the destruction of the Greeks. After that, it does not matter that Euripides' tragedy ends with the hopeless despair of the departure into exile and without restating the moral of the story. What is important is to strike hard, and indeed Poseidon does so: "Now you are going to pay. Wage war, stupid mortals, destroy fields and towns, desecrate the temples, the tombs, and torture the vanquished. It will destroy all of you" (*TW-S,* final scene).

In Euripides' play, Hecuba's last words express the vast, infinite weariness of hopeless despair: "Support me, Oh trembling legs, start walking, / carry me into a slave's life" (*TW* 1327–1328). By contrast, Sartre's Hecuba ends up as a rebel and a militant who shouts at the Greeks who drag her along: "take us, dogs, drag us away. We will not go willingly into exile and slavery" (*TW-S,* xi).

One could argue that these interventions radically transform the meaning of Euripides' tragedy. But Sartre clearly defends the "total nihilism" of his conclusion, and proclaims that he has taken what to the Greeks would have appeared to be "subtle contradiction" and converted it into "negation, rejection" on the assumption that, as outsiders, we would understand it better. Clearly, it did not bother him that what he calls contradiction might, rather, be the very ambiguity that constitutes tragedy itself, and, in order to demonstrate the "lesson of tragedy," he was willing to expunge its lyricism. He has little concern with the tragic genre in itself, since it is not tragedy that interests him in *The Trojan Women.* Nor, I would add, was he concerned with the reference to antiquity. For when Bernard Pingaud refers ironically at the start of his interview to "ancient theater fanatics" who "periodically attempt to revive" productions of a forgotten past and fail because "that theater, inspired by a religious conception of the world that has become completely foreign, is too far removed from us,"[20] Sartre neither confirms nor denies the assertions.

Today these very considerations are what strike us as dated, if not obsolete. It is true that more than thirty years have passed since the production of Sartre's *Trojan Women* and the interview with Pingaud, and it seems in fact that this quarter century has moved us further away from the Sartrian interpretation of *The Trojan Women* while bringing us closer to the Greek tragedy. There are several reasons for this. Some have to do with the state of the world (and whether we like it or not, we can no longer claim that the time for a religious view of the natural order is past), while others have to do with the state of the theater in France in the 1980s and 1990s; the ancient theater group of the Sorbonne has ceased to exist, and today's stagings of tragedy are not reconstitutions but authentic theatrical productions, numerous enough in the last decade to allow us to conclude that Greek tragedy as a genre has something to say to us.[21]

I must confess that in rereading Sartre's play I have not experienced the enthusiasm for it that I felt in 1965, and I have yet to explain why: the reasons for my lack of enthusiasm seem only incidentally personal, since they have as much to do with what is specifically Greek in the tragic genre as with the reception of tragedy today.

What the Mourning Voice
of Tragedy Tells Us

I have said that Greek tragedy has something to say to us today. Now I must explain what I mean by that and, in doing so, return definitively to the mourning voice of tragedy.

First it is essential to clear up an ambiguity: every translation of Greek tragedy for the theater must, in one way or another, acknowledge a difference; in other words, it becomes an adaptation. Every translator knows this firsthand. Nevertheless, not all gaps are alike. It is clear that, if a word-for-word translation of a tragic text can be respected only in terms of the highly demanding mode of distanced faithfulness, it is because the text's literal materiality is ultimately untranslatable.[22] But the essential point has to be spelled out: if the selected text is one belonging to a highly codified genre, it is important to respect its specificity, and even its spirit. By specificity, I mean the tone as well as the metrical structure of the play, in which the allocation of dialogue and lyric passages respectively is significant.

Attention to tone is not Sartre's primary consideration, concerned as he is first of all with a certain style—his own theatrical style—in which trivial phrases and petit-bourgeois speech, as we have seen, play a fairly significant role. The iambic trimeters of *The Trojan Women* anticipate Aristotle's definition of this type of verse by seeming to imitate contemporary speech as closely as possible; Euripides also knew how to punctuate his text with the antiquated expressions which Aristotle also mentioned and which, not being part of everyday speech, "produced an effect of elevation in elocution (*to mē idiōtikon*)"[23] But, more significant than tone, to use Sartre's own words, is his decision to avoid "oratorio," for the sake of a systematic quest for "dramatization." Such an effort may be more significant, but it is also presumably out of date, if not obsolete.

We can grant that an unslanted adaptation of the lyric passages of tragedy is impossible, since we no longer know how to direct a chorus or to integrate music and dance fully into the staging of a text. Still, the dominance of lyricism in Euripides' *Trojan Women* appears well suited to the task of making the impact of mourning felt, of a mourning that nothing can appease, not even the repetition of its own voice, nothing except its own enormity.

Indeed, it is no accident that, when analyzing the two grounding moments of lamentation for the dead (the exacerbated crisis of the *planctus* leading to the brink of madness, and the ritualized order that the funeral lamentation establishes, opening up a psychic state of dreamlike concentration), Ernesto De Martino finds *The Trojan Women* the best example of this process of ritualization. In the initial crisis, this process introduces a certain order of gestures and behavior; thus, De Martino notes that Hecuba, accompanying herself by rocking back and forth, (*TW* 100–101) inaugurates the lamentation which, out of bitter recognition of a crushing pain, turns into song, in the topical sense, a *thrēnos*, a lamentation.[24] The staging of mourning is certainly not limited to this moment in the play; it applies to the tragedy as a whole. For we recognize here all the resources available to tragedy for portraying the many features of mourning that constitute the fabric of *The Trojan Women*. These features, which will be our focus throughout this study of tragedy, include the repetition of interjections like *io, oimoi, amoi,* and *aiai;* the evocation of the *thrēnos,* designated by name or recognizable behind a noun like *ialemos;* the changing of hymns into sobs; the association of the Muse with the wailing song.[25]

It is precisely the repetitiveness of mourning that Sartre considered irrelevant to his own day. For a political activist and intellectual of the 1960s, that was probably true.

It is possible that, with *The Trojan Women* as well as with other Euripidean tragedies and those of Aeschylus and Sophocles, we owe our sense of proximity to the very *oratorio* structure that Sartre rejected in the text in order to emphasize the message of struggle. There may be many reasons why we can understand the mourning of the vanquished without having to know that the victorious Greeks, so much like ourselves, will ultimately be destroyed, but surely the principal reason is that we have shed forever our complete faith in third-world progress. We no longer believe, as Sartre did, that the advent of postcolonial regimes can produce a "new man," and for that reason among others, we no longer demand that tragedy become a weapon in the struggle. Instead, we can now discern other aspects that are just as fundamental as the political ones that have been overemphasized for the last thirty years, I feel, at the expense of other, more hidden, voices.

Finally, in a world where even fundamental divisions seem obscure, and where Manicheism is not a comfortable option, expressions of mourning have become, if not a weapon of war, at least the only weapon in a struggle that is unarmed, or hopeless. Today, grief is often the grief of mothers, like that of Hecuba and Andromache in *The Trojan Women;*[26] and since the list is too long to name them all, let me invoke only the silent demonstrations of the Argentinean mothers, the "madwomen of May Square" whose grieving march for justice has been followed by the entire world.

It is fair to wager that in the "oratorio" form it is now the oratorio itself that spectators will choose to understand. And we shall certainly not find cause for hope in the oratorio, but rather a long meditation on the aporias of a world convulsed by history.

Because tragedy, in this present time of uncertainty seems to me to provide so much to ponder, I should like to turn to the study of those features that in Athens, under the generic topic of mourning in tragedy, resist the omnipresent grip of politics. Let me say it boldly: Euripides' *Trojan Women* is both a political play *and* an oratorio.

[II]

THE THEATER OF DIONYSUS IS NOT IN THE AGORA

In which the reader learns that Greek tragedy is more than a controlled self-representation that the city-state chooses to reveal.

> Il n'y a qu'un Dionysos, tout au plus deux manifestations.
> [There is but one Dionysus, at most two manifestations.]
> NIETZSCHE, *La naissance de la tragédie*
> (fragments posthumes)

The theater of Dionysus is not in the Agora. What sounds at first like a simple statement is much more than that when we observe that in the civic space of city-states (*poleis*), the theater was generally located in the Agora, the most political of public places.[1] By making a distinction between theater and politics in this symbolic way, I wish to indicate from the outset a departure from the wholly political readings that have dominated studies of tragedy for several decades.[2] The comparison between a contemporary conception of tragedy—in this case the adaptation of *The Trojan Women* which Jean-Paul Sartre undertook during the 1960s—and Euripides' drama in which the mourning voice of tragedy is clearly heard (and as I have shown, tragedy has to be considered as *both* oratorio *and* political theater), forces us to take theater seriously, and, without subordinating it to politics, to understand tragedy as a whole, in its literary as well as its civic dimensions. To understand Greek tragedy we must first understand the *theatron*, in other words, theater as both a place and an assembled collectivity, occurring in civic space and time.

I repeat: the theater of Dionysus is not in the Agora. This statement by itself does not afford sufficient grounds for abandoning interpretations rooted in the reality of Athenian social practices in which the theater and the assembly contribute to the highly "political" function of public speech. But theater, tragic theater at least, was also—and perhaps best—equipped to deal with issues that the citizens of Athens preferred to reject or ignore. For evidence of this, I suggest we look at three richly symbolic sites: the theater of Dionysus, the Athenian Agora, and the hill of the Pnyx where, beginning in the fifth century B.C.E., the assembly (*ekklēsia*) convened.

The Agora, the Theater, the Pnyx

The fact that in Athens the Agora was probably the site of the earliest "theatrical" events[3] does not in itself set Athens apart from other city-states.[4] However, a specifically Athenian reorganization of the space occurred, probably at the beginning of the fifth century B.C.E. (shortly after Cleisthenes' reforms), in which the theater left the Agora—even though the latter's very name (from *ageiro,* to assemble) seems to indicate that its purpose was to accommodate all civic gatherings—and was established at the foot of the Acropolis, just as, in the final years of the sixth century, the assembly (*ekklēsia*) had left the Agora for the Pnyx. Thus, in the same way and at almost the same time, the assembly and the theater moved, a short distance but just far enough, outside the limits that the archaic city assigned to public life. Whether these two moves were simply for convenience[5] or resulted from some concerted political and intellectual strategy of the Cleisthenes era and its aftermath, the combination could very well have been due to more than random coincidence.[6] In both cases, it was clearly a matter of welcoming the *demos,* the reinforced and renewed *demos* that Cleisthenes sought to "mix together" (Aristotle, *Constitution of Athens,* 21, 2), in order to give it more effective power (*kratos*). As a result, although it did not lose its function of accommodating civic gatherings, the Agora was henceforth the site of more limited meetings (like the Council of Five Hundred, which was permanently installed in the *bouleuterion*) as well as more ritualized[7] and possibly, more politically symbolic ones.[8] Moreover, while certain theatrical presentations—such as the dances of cyclic choruses that accompanied the performance of the dithyrambs—continued to take place there,[9] nonetheless, the theater of Athens as such had left the Agora.

Thus, two aspects of a single event draw our attention. One is separation: instead of sharing the same space, the theater and the assembly each left the common site of all public events in order to go separately into a place of its own. The second is solidarity: both departed at the same time and as if in a single movement. We are left to determine which of these two facts is paramount. I have chosen to stress separation rather than solidarity not only because *politics is not theater,* but, and this is the essential point of this work, because tragedy is not *only* politics..

In Thucydides' *Histories,* book III, the Athenian politician Cleon states emphatically that politics is not theater.[10] Cleon was a demagogue or, as Aristotle calls him in the *Athēnaiōn Politeia,* "leader of the people." Thucydides did not like Cleon any more than Aristotle did, but there is no doubt that he has him speak in a manner appropriate for a popular leader to whom the *demos* listened.

Criticizing the usual procedures of the people's Assemblies, Cleon describes them as "jousts" (*agōnes*) organized by the Athenians (*agōnothetountes*), as if they involved winning prizes (*athla*); however, in these "jousts," citizens became passive spectators (*theatai*) of speech. Cleon specifically compares the Athenian assembly to an audience gathered to listen to sophists, and he does so—and this is what interests me—in a language equally appropriate for a theater audience,[11] which sees words but likes to hear actions.[12] We should not forget that Pericles himself, according to Thucydides, defended the seeing, *theasthai,* provided that its object was always the true power of the city-state.[13] However, although Cleon hardened the binary oppositions, he still showed himself to be a disciple of Pericles in that he valued reality (*ergon*) above all else, and his diagnosis of the way the assemblies worked—he claimed that Athenians responded (quite inappropriately) to the reality of facts by listening because the only thing they were willing to contemplate was speech (*logos*)—suggests that the most dangerous threat to politics was theatricality.

Here a question arises: what do we make of assemblies that were actually and institutionally held in the theater?[14] A first example raises no major difficulties: it concerns the assembly that the Athenians held each year in the theater of Dionysus a few days after the Great Dionysia—the day after the Pandia festival, to be exact—to examine how well the performance of the ceremony conformed to the tradition.[15] This comes as no surprise. Since theater was a civic event, the performance of theatrical productions was of the utmost concern to the Athenian city-state, and one assembly was held specifically for the purpose of examining any misdeeds and violations that might have impaired the proper functioning of the festival. But, because theater was a separate entity to be handled separately, this assembly took place in the theater of Dionysus and not, as would other assemblies, on the Pnyx.

Other examples are more ambiguous, or more difficult to analyze, but we learn more from them about what may—and may not—be done in the theater. Here we are sometimes dealing with assemblies in the strictest sense, but also quite often with what I shall call civic scenes that took place not on the Pnyx, in an *ekklēsia,* but in the theater itself, during the Great Dionysia, before the dramatic contests began. Such events are thus both distinct from the theatrical presentations themselves and drawn into their orbit. While I do not intend to provide an exhaustive summary of the analyses recently done by others about the civic dimension of the Great Dionysia,[16] I shall mention a few that are particularly relevant for my thesis. In the second half of the fourth century B.C.E., the theater of Dionysus appears to have become the obligatory context for all ceremonies awarding citizens crowns for bravery.[17] Aeschines protested against the practice, claiming that a crown awarded by the people should be presented at the Pnyx, in the assembly of the people, among Athenians alone, and not before the mixed audience of the theater, composed of foreigners as well as citizens; his testimony may not be entirely reliable, however, since the winner of the crown was Demosthenes, whom the Athenians had chosen at the suggestion of another Athenian, Ctesiphon.[18] One suspects that Demosthenes' point of view in this case was quite different, since his self-interest was at stake, and indeed he had no difficulty justifying the choice of the theater as the right place for pedagogy in action, where those who heard about worthy deeds (*hoi akousantes*) could learn to imitate them.[19]

Still another civic event, also an integral part of the Great Dionysia, is particularly noteworthy because it links several essential moments in the life of the city-state. This was the presentation of the war orphans in the theater, just before the start of the competition (*agōn*) among tragedies. Though it did not take place during an assembly of the people, this ceremony certainly recalls yet another assembly held in the theater, during which—at the midpoint of the two-year ephebate—the ephebes passed in review.[20] What interests me most is that the orphan ceremony was both the necessary preamble to the tragic contests[21] and the deferred conclusion of this appropriation of private mourning into civic ritual, which the public funeral rite initiates in a number of ways. The evocation of this presentation of the orphans in the theater is a *topos* of political rhetoric[22] that confirms the symbolic importance of such an event. But whatever the strategy for relying on this *topos,* fourth-century orators seem to have agreed to recall this ceremony in the past tense, as if the practice had ended[23] at the end of the fifth century, the end of the golden age of tragedy, and this point merits a closer look.

It was, in the rather dramatic words of Aeschines, the evocation of a blessed past:

> Once, at a time when the city was better governed . . . on this very day and at the moment when, as now, the tragedies were to be presented, the herald came forward and introduced the orphans whose fathers had died in battle . . . and the most beautiful speeches were made, the very best an incentive to valor. (*Against Ctesiphon*, 154)

To this Aeschines compared the present disaster:

> Imagine for a moment that you are in the theater and that you see the herald coming forward and someone is about to make a speech as decreed (by Ctesiphon), and ask yourself if the relatives of the dead will shed more tears for the tragedies and the suffering of the heroes (*epi tais tragōidiais kai tois hērōikois pathesi*) that are about to be presented on stage than for the ingratitude of the city. [24]

We should remember that this was a time when "the man who made the children orphans"—that is, Demosthenes—was being glorified. The parents of the dead would thus have every reason to weep over the ingratitude of the city, and Aeschines formally cries shame—hence this evocation of an institution in grave danger. But, above and beyond rhetorical exaggeration, the speech is, between the lines, a kind of reflection on the articulation between the tragic representation and the shift of private mourning into a service, and then into a civic celebration. The orator says in essence that in better times, when government was good, the private sorrow of the orphans' families (*oikeioi*) always evolved into recognition of the generosity of the city; and, as spectators, those families were ready to "pour out their tears" (*dakrua aphēsein*) over the heroes' suffering; but it must be understood that those tears, shed over misfortunes that did not touch individuals directly, were supposed to complete what had begun with the herald's political proclamation concerning the orphans. Indeed, these very specific spectators are purged by their tears of any remaining private mourning (*oikeion*). In short, the city had two means of urging the families of the dead to transcend their personal grievances: first, through political sublimation, and adherence to civic idealism; and second, through forgetting, releasing all sadness through tears shed for the suffering of others.

Impersonal tears to expel private suffering? One might argue against this assumption that Aeschines is an implausible theoretician of tragic purification, even more so of tragic purgation (*katharsis*), and that we should not read too much into his words. But, in fact, it is enough at this point simply to grant that, in this passage of *Against Ctesiphon,* there is, above and beyond the requisite indignation, a close correlation between the tragic effect and the expression of mourning.

Now we are firmly situated in the theater, and not in the socio-historical margins of the *theatron.* And here we shall remain, in order to try to appreciate what makes, or does not make, tragedy a stage for Athenian politics.

A Political Stage?

For several decades, it has seemed as though those who adhere to a concept of theater as an Athenian *institution* were convinced that theater—in this case tragedy—is thoroughly political, and, I might add, civic and democratic as well. The same can be said of comedy, though we are not concerned with Aristophanes here. To support their position, these scholars turn to a long list of examples that always begins with mention of the role of the Archon, the organizer of the Great Dionysia who designated the *choregoi* for the tragic productions. After reminding us that, along with the trierarchy, the choregia was the most important civic service, the experts nonetheless hasten to note that theater was an amusement reserved for citizens: all of its participants were Athenian, from the poet who taught the men, *hebontes,*[25] to the actors and *choreutai,*[26] the latter constituting a pacifist version of citizen-soldiers,[27] and including the spectators—the *theatron*—whose placement in the stands amounted to a sort of "map of the civic body,"[28] and to the judges of the dramatic contest, recruited from among the ten tribes of Cleisthenes, as were the ten generals (*strategoi*) whose solemn offerings opened the tragic performance.[29]

It takes but one more step to turn the *theatron,* a gathering of citizens, into a barely distinguishable double of the assembly (*ekklēsia*),[30] momentarily "forgetting"—as Attic orators never forgot—that the presence of foreigners (not to mention the controversial question of the presence of women) was characteristic of this particular type of assembly.[31]

To avoid risking such simplifications, which arise from a too obvious desire to wholly "politicize" everything Athenian, we have no choice but to consider the relationship between the *theatron* and the texts it welcomed on stage. However much the civic character of the theater is stressed, we have to recognize the profound ambiguity in the fact that theatrical performance was at once a civic event and also quite open to noncivic features. This is the reason why Pierre Vidal-Naquet points out quite emphatically the difference between a production of tragedy and a session of the *ekklēsia* and at the same time, moving from the *theatron* to the *orkhēstra,* reminds us that the chorus members, contrary to an oversimplified analysis that makes the chorus an embodiment of the people, rarely play the roles of citizens;[32] moreover, while the chorus may see itself as adviser to the hero, its advice is rarely followed, so rarely that dialogue, in the tragic universe, is often thwarted.[33] As for the hero, even if he speaks the Attic dialect, and if the iambic meter lends his language a certain quality of ordinariness, as Aristotle maintains, his action can only "displace, overturn, and sometimes suppress the political order." In other words, the tragic universe is everything but a replica of the city—which Vidal-Naquet characterizes as being "in its very structure an anti-tragic machine."[34]

A better approach is to move resolutely to the very space of representation in order to examine the texts themselves, all that remain to us of the long days citizens spent at the theater. To go straight to the point, I shall begin by asking, almost at random, what the *polis* might have made of a tragedy such as Sophocles' *Electra.*

Mourning Becomes Electra

A few very brief remarks will suffice to illustrate my point: they constitute the basis for one example, which I have chosen because it raises with singular relevance the question of politics in tragedy. I am referring to *Choephori,* the penultimate drama of the *Oresteia.* The protagonist is Electra, who has lost her father and wishes to be rid of her mother Clytemnestra as well, since Clytemnestra had killed her husband Agamemnon when he returned from Troy. Electra's mourning can only be transformed into revenge. For Aeschylus, who did not name his tragedy *Electra* after its heroine, revenge—Clytemnestra's assassination by her son Orestes—is only one moment of tragic action measured against the trilogy as a whole, the *Oresteia*, and that moment is symmetrical with Agamemnon's murder by his wife, Clytemnestra, in the preceding tragedy, the *Agamemnon*. Justice (*Dikē*) against Justice, Ares against Ares,[35] under the sign of the *anti-;* by definition, nothing is finished because time progresses only through repetition. One might say this time is characteristic of tragedy, except for the fact that the tragic action does not come to an end, and we have to wait for the *Eumenides* to provide its conclusion by making the Athenian *polis* the ultimate recourse. This is certainly the ultimate lesson that Euripides, in his sarcastic fashion, retains from this story, the final part of the trilogy. From the mouth of the *Dioscuri* comes the emphatic announcement that Orestes and his sister must leave Argos forever for Athens, concluding a plot in which virtually all values have been reversed, beginning with Electra's hatred, which fed on itself and collapsed once the murder was committed, a murder she had ardently desired and in which she was an active participant.

Electra's situation is very different in Sophocles' play by that name. In the first place she embodies a permanent threnody, or lamentation,[36] which, according to the orthodoxy of civic performances as expressed in official speech such as a funeral oration,[37] would necessarily be subject to the harshest condemnation—and indeed, it is in the name of a coherent criticism of her self-indulgent lamentation that the chorus women gently reproach Electra for her excessive mourning. In fact, by stressing the excessive nature of this uncontrollable mourning expressed in terms of "forever" (*aei*), the text suggests the strength of the potential threat that Electra's behavior, characterized by her pointed rejection of amnesty, poses to the values of the city-state.[38]

However, nothing in Sophocles' *Electra* is simply univocal. For the present, I shall simply point out the less than edifying nature of this tragedy, far removed from the didactic aim that so many contemporary readers attribute to the tragic genre as did the Aeschylus depicted in Aristophanes' *Frogs*.

While the chorus women fault Electra for her tireless, unshakable grief, they do so in the spirit of the precept "nothing in excess," bringing to the foreground the limitations in the human condition. While it is certainly not immaterial that Electra comes to refer to the women by the rarest of terms, "citizenesses" (*politides*),[39] she does so because they are the most reliable of allies for Agamemnon's daughter and because, rejoicing at having just found Orestes again, she readily identifies her cause with that of the city-state, which means that she does away with all politics in the implementation of her own vengeance.[40] Truly, however, Electra never ceased ensuring that association, since, from the very beginning of the play, though calling for the ultimate penalty, murder, for Agamemnon's murderers (*antiphonous dikas,* 246), she was claiming pity (*aidōs*) and piety (*eusebeia*), in terms that clearly echo *The Eumenides* concerning *aidōs* and *sebas,* though in a way that is completely regressive in relation to Aeschylus's tragedy. For there it is precisely this definition of justice as vengeance that Athena wishes to move beyond when she commits the Areopagus to the observance of morality and fear so dear to the Erinyes; the Areopagus meets and acquits Orestes, judging his mother's crime to have offset his own.[41]

But—and this is what gives to the tragedy its corrosive power—there is no sequel to Sophocles' *Electra,* not only because the play is not part of a trilogy, and, unlike *Choephori,* has neither conclusion nor correction beyond itself, but also because no future is included within it,[42] not even potentially, and definitely not in the form of a declaration made by some *deus ex machina. Electra* is essentially *Choephori* without the *Eumenides:* time immobilized in the *anti-* of vengeance, which is identified with justice and, as such, endowed with the *kratos* that is reserved in the *Oresteia* for Zeus Agoraios[43]—but, as we know, the theater is no longer in the Agora . . . hence we are not surprised when, a few lines further on in the same *stasimon,* Erinys becomes another name for justice, *Dikē.*[44] The chorus women still believe in justice, whatever name it is given, but they begin to doubt whether Electra believes in it when, seeing her wholly given over to hatred during her confrontation with Clytemnestra, they confess: "I see that she is filled with fury; but, as to whether she is being just, I no longer see that she cares" (610–611).

Later in the plot, as I have already indicated, Electra refers to her companions as "citizenesses" (*politides*), employing the surprising feminine form of the noun in Greek, so rare, so improbable in fifth-century texts that it is not by chance that Euripides refers to it in his own *Electra.*[45] There should no longer be any doubt that what Sophocles' *Electra* presents in the *theatron,* signaled by interminable mourning and vengeance, is a woman's politics, even a "politics in the feminine"—impossible in Greece, and yet presented—where fury has replaced *logos.* Once the murder is committed, the tragedy can end. "I cannot blame you,"[46] says the chorus to Orestes after the murder of Clytemnestra, and Orestes has no sooner entered the palace to kill Aegisthus than the brief song of triumph and joy erupts, punctuating the *exodos:*

O seed of Atreus, you have suffered so much
with difficulty you come at last to freedom,
Perfected (*teleōthen*) by the day's achievement.
(Sophocles, *Electra*, 1508–1510)

Teleōthen is the last word of the tragedy, as if to emphasize that the end is indeed final,[47] without the sinister connotations that in *Agamemnon* associated the consequences of *telos* with the performing of a brutal murder or a corrupt sacrifice.[48] In short, the story ends, and everything suggests that it is not an edifying tale.

At this point in my argument I could—and perhaps I should—list everything that, in the tragic genre, while close to the political, could be called *antipolitical*. I will explain my choice of this term in Chapter III, but for now it suffices to say that it can designate the other of politics, but also another politics, no longer based on consensus and living together, but on what I call the "bond of division."[49] Adopting once again the ultimately external point of view of the historian of Athenian society, I can at last return to the theater of Dionysus in order to situate there certain assemblies that openly deviate from civic and democratic norms of Athens, because they fall directly under the heading of "the bond of division."

In the Theater of Dionysus, Seditious Assemblies

Turning to some extreme examples, we shall recall that the theatrical space dedicated to Dionysus ought to be a protected and protecting place within the city. Whereas the regular performance of theatrical productions in the secular realm of the city-state is synonymous with an era of peace,[50] the chaos during periods of discord is acted out in the very real murders committed in the theater. We owe the accounts of such episodes to historiographical writing. These acts, monstrous in the eyes of the historians as an indication that the city-state was beset by civil war (*stasis*), were all the more horrifying when they took place in Dionysus's space.

According to Xenophon, at the beginning of the fourth century the enemies of the Corinthian aristocrats, with "the most impious of intentions" (since they exploited the celebration of the *Eukleia* [beautiful glory] to massacre their enemies), began a slaughter in the Agora, killing indiscriminately "the man standing in the middle of a group, or seated, or in the theater and even the judges in the middle of deliberating"; such bloodshed, even in the midst of a civil war, was perceived as a shocking sacrilege (*asebeia*).[51] Thucydides, as we might expect, described the *stasis* best in his paradigmatic digression on the horrors of Corcyra. The historian recounts the horrors, telling of men who "shrank from nothing" and "went to even worse lengths" such as fathers killing their sons[52] and the slaughter of people praying in temples where they had sought refuge, and culminating with "some [who] were even walled up in the temple of Dionysus and died there."[53] By all accounts this was shocking because the theater represented, or was supposed to represent, both as a place and as a civic institution, the practice of consensus that the civic ideology considered the essential quality of political life.

However, I mention these bloody incidents only as a reminder, and I want to conclude with the meetings held in the precinct of Dionysus during the *stasis,* the time of civil war. The first step in the handover of power to the Thirty Tyrants was an assembly held in the theater of Dionysus at Mounikhia.[54] Was the site chosen simply for reasons of convenience, because the theater of Piraeus was smaller than the Pnyx and the entire *demos* could not be accommodated there? This is the usual explanation for this choice, which modern historians compare to the choice of the sanctuary of Poseidon at Colonus when, in 412–411, the conspirators hostile to democracy sought to have an assembly (*ekklēsia*) ratify the transformation of Athens into an oligarchical regime "democratically."[55]

As long as we are making analogies, however, we should be consistent and recall another assembly, one held in 411 B.C.E. in the theater of Mounikhia. This assembly was as irregular as the preceding one, but its conclusion was exactly the opposite, since this time it ended with the oligarchy of the Four Hundred.[56] I should add that this assembly in the theater of Dionysus at Piraeus led to the return of the hoplites into the city and to a meeting in the sanctuary of the *Dioscuri* where the only decision taken was to hold another assembly later in the precinct of Dionysus—a real one, as it were, since it would be *peri homonoias*— (about concord).[57] Something happened to prevent this assembly from taking place and instead the Athenians actually met on the Pnyx,[58] which suggests that we should look for an explanation for all these facts that is not simply conjectural.

We notice first that Dionysus, whether in his own theater or not (though quite often it was in that space), receives assemblies that can be called liminal, gatherings that have to do with passage from one thing to another, from democracy to oligarchy, or vice versa, and that they are usually held against a background of civic troubles. We might say that a Dionysian space, if it is sacred (*hieron*),[59] is paradoxically all the more able to confer legitimacy to the new order that it is in the process of fashioning; moreover, by the very nature of the god who inhabits the place, it constitutes an "alien" enclave inside the territory of the city into which it is nevertheless fully integrated. What the traitors of 412 had opted for, in choosing Poseidon's temple at Colonus, if we are to credit a fleeting reference in Thucydides (VIII, 67, 2), was a site exterior to the *polis, exō poleōs,* outside the city certainly, since, for the Athenian historian, *polis* is more than once used as a substitute for *astu,* the entire urban area. But every substitution can be reversed, and if *polis* can often mean *astu,* it is because, between the urban area and the city-state, the relationship in Athens is one of close solidarity. Clearly, what the oligarchs were trying to do in 412, as in 404, was to get outside the city-state and the civic organization that too often were identified with democracy.

It is not surprising to find that politics does not change without a change of location in a civilization in which places are never neutral, but rather invested with mythico-religious meaning. Nor does the fact that the overthrow of politicians occurred quite regularly by authority of Dionysus come as a surprise. Though all the gods were believed to be present at tragic performances in the *theatron* by their intermediaries, the priests, installed in places of honor around the priest of Dionysus Eleuthereus, it was important that Dionysus be alone in receiving an assembly when the city shook on its very foundations. We must acknowledge, however, that Dionysus enjoyed the turmoil of politics, since the very notion of "Dionysian politics," which may sound like an oxymoron,[60] presupposes a profound alteration, even a political metamorphosis. After that, how could anyone continue to claim that tragedy, by taking place in the theater of Dionysus, assumes a "predominantly" political character?

[III]

TRAGEDY AND THE ANTIPOLITICAL

*In which the reader measures how tragedy, as opposed to civic discourse,
expresses ineffable grief by means of the oratorio.*

> "Always," *aei*.
>> THE FIRST WORD OF SOPHOCLES' *Ajax*,
>>> spoken by Athena

> You are my own, my sister, Ismene.
>> ANTIGONE'S FIRST LINE, Sophocles' *Antigone*

> "Ah me, ah wretched me!"
>> ELECTRA'S FIRST SPEECH, Sophocles' *Electra* (77)

Tragedy, as I have said in the preceding chapter, is antipolitical. Let me
explain this term, which I felt I needed to coin since the existing term,
a-political, conveys a notion of indifference or neutrality rather than one
of active opposition to the political.

In brief, I will argue that any behavior that diverts, rejects, or threatens, consciously or not, the obligations and prohibitions constituting the
ideology of the city-state (which in turn creates and maintains civic ideology), is antipolitical. By "ideology of the city-state"[1] I mean, essentially, the idea that the city-state must be—and so, by definition is—*one
and at peace* with itself.[2] While the formula "must be, and therefore is"
seems faulty in that it postulates a curious logical sequence, I wish to
suggest that the confusion between the factual and the ideal inherent in
imaginary formulations is one of the constitutive and even vital principles of civic ideology. However, another of these principles—even
more fundamental, perhaps, although it is a corollary of the first—is the
forgetting of conflict, or, more precisely, of the inherently conflictual
nature of politics. I have already had occasion to describe the function-

ing of the city-state's political memory, which resembles a consistent practice of forgetting,[3] and I would refer the reader to these analyses.

"Antipolitical" can mean two very different things, depending upon whether we define politics as a practice of consensus—currently the most widely accepted definition—or instead define politics, beginning with the Athenian democracy during the most fertile period of the tragic genre, as essentially conflictual, with the conflict almost always repressed. What I called Electra's "politics of the feminine" in the preceding chapter could not be called political according to the first definition: in this case the attitudes that actually exceed civic order and thereby threaten it are characterized as antipolitical. In terms of the second definition, any behavior that rejects the ordinary functioning of the city-state is antipolitical; it claims to be authentically political, but in an oppositional mode, one policy as opposed to another.

I realize that the difference I want to elucidate here between these two senses of the word—the political other and another politics—is not easily demonstrated, whether the latter is presented as an alternative or simply imagined. I will no doubt find myself often working close to the boundary between these two orders, and even confusing them. But we must accept this difficulty if we wish to understand tragedy, to hear its voice. There is an open conflict in the tragic genre between the two opposing, or more exactly, competing, meanings of "always" (*aei*).

Aei versus *aei:* Aspects of a Conflict

"Always" is the standard, though imperfect, translation given for the adverb *aei*. If, however, we wish to examine the meaning of this term more closely, Emile Benveniste's essay "Expression indo-européenne de l'immortalité"[4] on the notion of *aiōn* sheds vivid light on the subject. After explaining how we can "derive the idea of the eternal" from the concept of "human age," and thus elevating an essentially temporal notion to intemporality, Benveniste turns to the convergence between *aiōn*, defined as designating primarily the "vital force," and adverbs derived from related forms that in the neuter mean "always": thus he observes that

this always designates something that is perpetually beginning anew, before becoming a permanent and immobile always.

{27}

However, the definition of *aiōn* that Benveniste gives later is even more suggestive, for it illuminates the uses of the adverb *aei* in a political context. *Aiōn* is a force that is

> single and double . . . transitory and permanent, running out and being reborn in the course of generations, destroying itself in its renewal and subsisting forever in its endlessly beginning finitude.

When he adds that

> the life force, implying unceasing recreation of the principle that nourishes life, suggests to the mind a compelling image of something that maintains itself without end, in the freshness of the always new,

we cannot help recalling one of the possible figures of the city-state in Aristotle, conceived of in book III of *The Politics* as remaining one and the same,

> although it is true that all the time some are dying and others being born, just as it is our custom to say that a river or a spring is the same river or spring although one stream of water is always being added to it and another being withdrawn from it.[5]

It is true that Aristotle indicates a qualification when he adds, "the people are the same people for the similar reason of continuity," but I disagree with those modern readers who translate *genos* as "race"; and in fact it is doubtless in the context of autochthony that such a definition derives its full meaning. Consider two of Thucydides' pronouncements on Athenian autochthony, in contrast to the heterogeneity of the populations of most city-states:

> Always (*aei*) [i.e., generation after generation] the same men inhabited Attica.

> Our ancestors . . . , by dwelling in this country always (*aei*) in succession from generation to generation, handed it down to us.[6]

Since it falls to *aei* to denote the permanence of the Athenian principle through the ages, the most obviously political usage of this adverb can be observed in formula-like designations of magistrates, for example *ton aiei en arkhēi ontōn*,[7] "those who hold power time after time," meaning year after year, in an obvious allusion to the rotation of offices through which, repeatedly and without interruption, magistrates succeeded one another in the civic exercise of power, the *arkhē.* "Without interruption" is probably the most precise meaning of the adverb in the domain of politics, where it implies a constructive repetition in unbroken continuity. Thus, *The Constitution of Athens* refers to the eleventh and last change in the text of the city-state's constitution, a revolution in the same radical sense the term acquired in the 1793 Convention in France, even though that term itself would have been inconceivable for fifth-century Athenians. This change (*metabolē*) in the Athenian constitution, which saw the people triumph over the Thirty Tyrants and seize control of the city, led to the prevailing form of government "by always attributing more freedom to the majority."[8] In this description, the term *aei* suggests a progression through repetition within sameness, within a politics whose measures, all of which are directed toward the same end, are on every occasion as it were a renewal and a reaffirmation of the principle of democracy.

However, recourse to *aei* clearly proves most effective—performative somehow, an incantation, in any case—when some temporal break has occurred in the life of a city-state; the term is used to suggest that, in and by means of the succession of the archons, beyond the vicissitudes that have shaken its unity (during the time of the Thirty Tyrants, people spoke of "sorrows" [*sumphorai*]), what is being perpetuated is the city-state itself, one and always the same. It is true that, to someone who believes in the unchanging nature of the city-state, a situation of this last type can prove problematic, and it is indeed problematic for Aristotle in book III of *The Politics.* Here, reflecting on changes of constitution within a city-state, Aristotle does not view as self-evident the idea that identity can be maintained throughout the random events of history.[9] It is possible, however, that the operation that aims to construct identity from the multiple and diverse time of historical processes constitutes precisely the most current definition of politics in its effectiveness, in that it offers the city-state the model of the repetitive, natural regularity of (and this is the important part) the succession of generations.

This regularity is not absent from tragedy, to be sure, although tragedy situates it in the past from the standpoint of a present catastrophe—thus when the chorus in *Ajax* observes that with the exception of the fallen hero, the *aiōn* of the *Aiaikidai* (in other words the vital force of the Aeacidae, the descendants of Aeachus, including Achilles and Ajax) has never "nourished" such a calamity,[10] or when the messenger in *The Persians* announces that "those who always held the first rank in their loyalty to the leader" (meaning servants of the great king, whose rank was passed on from father to son) died wretchedly.[11] This use of *aei* may also be more openly civic when, for example, it involves expressing in the future a law that is actually in effect in contemporary Athens;[12] or when, in *Antigone*, the tyrant Creon specifically characterizes the old men in the chorus as those who "always honor the power of the throne of Laius"[13]—a way for the new king to emphasize their fidelity to the tyranny throughout the rifts that have led from Laius to Oedipus, to Oedipus's sons, and then to Creon himself; or when, at the end of Euripides' *Suppliant Women*, Theseus invites the Argives to honor Athens by transmitting the memory of its kindnesses endlessly, from generation to generation.[14] However, the most simply positive use of *aei*, "always," is the one that serves to mark the praise of a city-state that has remained eternally faithful to its founding laws.[15]

Yet, aside from these few instances, the tragic genre generally reserves *aei* for other purposes. In Greek tragedy, "always" belongs not to human beings, but to "all powerful Time," which in *The Suppliant Women* Euripides calls "ancient father," *palaios patēr*.[16] Nor should we forget the gods: their existence is regulated by the timeless temporality of *aei,* which is also that of the cult that men dedicate to them; but their interventions in human life cannot fail to disrupt human temporality repeatedly.[17] Thus mortals experience their lives in the form of chance (*tukhē*); for them, "always" means only the recurrence of life's vicissitudes.[18] It is all but unthinkable that "the gods' time and men's time"[19] can ever be interconnected, even though in an altogether exceptional way the end of the *Oresteia* seems to realize the dream of rooting politics in the divine *aei,* thanks to the installation in Athens of the Erinyes, who have become benevolent Eumenides.[20] Still, as I have already indicated, this is an exception in the tragic genre, where it is obvious that *aei,* "always," does not belong to men.

Accordingly, it is probably reasonable to hypothesize that a fixation on *aei* will be, for every tragic hero, the disquieting indication of a latent and poorly controlled passion—one has only to think of Hippolytus's claim to be living always at Artemis's side, and of the way he emphatically declares that "always" women are women (Euripides, *Hippolytus,* 17, 664–668), or to recall Orestes stating proudly that he would always keep on killing "evil women" (Euripides, *Orestes,* 1590); Phaedra is one of them, and rightly one of the best known; she ought to be, and I am resolutely on Orestes' side, from Euripides to Racine. But of all the tragic authors, Sophocles is the one who put this obsession most explicitly at the center of his work, and the madness of his heroes—if one can call rigid indeterminability, like that of Antigone or Ajax, madness— often lies in a belief that human affairs are governed by *aei*.

The same is true of Deianira: no matter what this unhappy wife does, her good intentions are always doomed by the quarrel swirling around her: a quarrel that is her destiny, inscribed in her very name—"the one whom quarrels surround, always Deianira" (*tan amphineike Deianeiran aei*).[21] It is also true of Antigone, who subsumed all human time in the endless duration of Hades, and of Oedipus, whom Creon rightly describes as always yielding to anger (*Oedipus at Colonus*, 855).

It is above all true of Ajax, and I would argue that it is no coincidence that *aei* is the first word of the tragedy of which he is the eponymous hero: "Always hunting, son of Laertes, always looking for a way to surprise your enemies!" Similarly, *menis*, wrath, is one of the first words of *The Iliad* ("Sing, goddess, the wrath of Achilles") and *aner*, man, is one of the first words of *The Odyssey* ("Tell me, muse, of the man of many devices"). There are two differences, however, which cannot be ignored. The first is that "wrath" and "man" are objects, declined in the accusative case, when they are used in the opening sentences of the epics, while the adverb *aei, aiei, aien,* is immutable, like that which it designates, owing to its neuter form. The second, more troubling difference stems from the consummate art with which Sophocles tends to blur things. The initial "always" spoken by Athena does not characterize Ajax (in retrospect, perhaps, surprising), but rather, Odysseus. It is true that on this occasion the goddess, moved by her own hatred, is gravely mistaken in attributing to her protégé her own exacerbated feelings, which are indeed those of Ajax as well but which, with typical prudence, Odysseus carefully avoids in himself. If anyone in this tragedy really suffers from *aei* as from a passion or a disease,[22] it is Ajax, who is maddened by rage when he is unable to don Achilles' armor, which Odysseus has appropriated. At the height of his madness (*mania*), the hero believes that he can always count on his alliance with Athena (*Ajax*, 117). When he comes to his senses, struck down but still enraged, he does not give up his belief in *aei*, and when he seems finally to acknowledge that for human beings everything is transitory—that, for example, all-powerful sleep does not always exercise its hold over men (674–675)[23] and that friendship and hatred are not bound to last "always"

(678–682)—it is the clearest indication that he is actually taking pains to speak untruthfully in order to elude the vigilance of those around him. Every passion lives by claiming for itself *aei*, "always," as its temporality, and of all the passions, hatred is without doubt the most violent. In Sophocles' tragedy, it is Ajax who hates Odysseus, and not the reverse, and just as Athena is mistaken, so is the hero when he believes he can credit his enemy with the "always" of hatred.[24] There is a difference, however, in that the mistake of a goddess has no consequences, whereas Ajax falls victim to his own hatred, manipulated "from above" by Athena.

We can identify yet another Sophoclean protagonist who endlessly conjugates passion in the mood of *aei:* I am referring, of course, to Electra, whose passion is mourning. So let us return to the case of Agamemnon's daughter.

Electra, Again and Always

Is it because mourning is repetitive—and the race of women seems doomed to repeat itself endlessly[25]—that women love mourning so much? A scene in Euripides' *Andromache* affirms this when Hector's widow, the concubine of Neoptolemus, observes that "woman is so made that she charms her present evils by having them always on her lips" (*Andromache,* 94–95).

Electra, not yet a grown woman, is in mourning for her father, and plotting her revenge, like the Erinyes whom she in some way imitates, within the limits of her mortality. And like the avenging goddesses,[26] she too is constantly associated with *aei;* the adverb is used in connection with her at least fifteen times in the play, and not including the occasions when Clytemnestra diverts the word for her own use. Electra is associated with "always" because mourning for her takes the form of fury, a fury in no way diminished by tears, a "too sorrowful anger" (*huperalge kholon*), says the chorus.[27] In addition, she identifies with the nightingale, a bird that was once a woman and that forever sings its lament for the dead son;[28] and, moreover, her most crucial statement, based on a double negation, concerns a refusal to forget ("there is no question that I may ever forget," she repeats in answer to the objurgations of the chorus, which urges her to exercise restraint).[29] There is still more to be said on the *aei* of Electra in terms of the use of this adverb to refer to the connotations of *aiōn* found in Benveniste's study. When the chorus affirms that Electra "endlessly gives birth to wars against her own life" (*sai dusthumōi tiktous' aiei / psukhai polemous*),[30] how can we miss the latent contradiction in such a description, when *aei,* derived from a root that means vital force, is twisted to serve a sterile birth? Because the continuous generation to which Electra—*a-lektra,* literally, without a bed—devotes all her energies is the pure repetition of giving birth to pain and tears, just as in *The Trachiniae,* it is always by nourishing "one fear after another" (*aei tin' ek phobou phobon trephō*)[31] that Deianira exhausts her energy. The *aei* of perpetual recreation is diverted to mourning, the nourishing and procreative feminine force is diverted to the service of sorrow, an endlessly revived and rejuvenated sorrow. When we observe that Sophocles' text occasionally inserts *aiōn,* the vital force, among its many uses of *aei,*[32] the full extent of the diversion becomes perhaps even more apparent.

For unlike mothers in tragedy mourning the death of a child, the promise of a vanished future, Electra weeps endlessly for her father. As Clytemnestra says, without real bitterness:

> It is in your nature, daughter, to always prefer your father.
> It must be said. Some children take their father's side
> While others love their mothers more.
> (Euripides, *Electra,* 1101–1104)

In Sophocles' tragedy, however, it seems that Clytemnestra, faced with a daughter immured in mourning, is not always this calm, at least according to Electra, who says her mother goes on speaking to her this way, day after day:

> Accursed creature, whom the gods detest. Are you the
> only one whose father is dead? Does no other mortal mourn?
> (Sophocles, *Electra,* 287–288)

As a counterpoint to this speech, I should like to cite Claudius's words to Hamlet:

{33}

> You must know your father lost a father,
> That father lost, lost his, and the survivor bound
> In filial obligation for some term
> To do obsequious sorrow. But to persevere
> In obstinate condolement is a course
> Of impious stubbornness. 'Tis unmanly grief.
>
> (Shakespeare, *Hamlet*, I, ii)

Not that, in this lesson in wisdom, Claudius's arguments are any better than Clytemnestra's, and indeed perhaps these two murderers are both particularly ill suited to remind their victims' children of the eternal truths about the mortality of fathers. The Argive women of the chorus, however, are much less dubious when they preach to Electra on this subject. Significantly, they state with perfect clarity what is concealed in this fierce and obstinate rejection of forgetting: a repetitive denegation of death, man's destiny as mortal (*brotos*) and therefore, strictly speaking, made of death. Well before Clytemnestra's words are spoken, the chorus has already put Electra on her guard: "you are not the only mortal, child, who has seen suffering" (Sophocles, *Electra,* 154). And before Electra's immense despair when she is deprived of the ashes of the false Orestes, they insist: "You are the child of a mortal father, Electra, remember, and Orestes was mortal; so do not lament too much! We must all bow to such fate" (Sophocles, *Electra,* 1171–1173).

To whom, then, is this solemn reminder of human mortality addressed? To Electra, no doubt, but it is not certain that she can hear it, since when the chorus teaches her this lesson she is actually living the final moments of her mourning. Immediately following the speech by the women of Argos, Orestes, deeply affected by his sister's grief, reveals his identity and tears give way to cries of joy, but they do not cause Electra, isolated in her happiness, to reflect reasonably on her mortality or on its dual nature. Are we to assume, then, that the one to whom the message is directed is none other than the spectator, mortal and citizen? If so, it is perhaps because the Athenian city-state, while presenting itself to citizens in the rhetoric of funeral orations as the sole embodiment of immortality and strictly limiting the length of time accorded the family for lamentation, distrusted the paralyzing seduction of mourning and the pleasure taken in immortalizing the voluptuousness of tears. Indeed, by voicing this harangue, perhaps the chorus women are *politides,* citizenesses, in a more civic sense than it first seemed. Still, this is not the last word of the tragedy, and the lesson may well be forgotten well before the *exodos*.

Thus, for the spectators the bewitched memory of the intractable *aei*, "always," unallied with wisdom, will surely be stronger than any moral lesson—all the more so as the curious impulse which regularly brings the tragic genre back to the multiform evocation of the despairing *aei* of mourning is coupled with the perceptible and even sensual sonorous pleasure that the ear is invited to enjoy when tragedy intensifies *aei* into *aiai*.

Aei, aiei, aiai

Sophocles' Electra might afford sufficient proof that loss is never better expressed than in the mode of "always," perhaps because it expects at least to reclaim eternity for itself, except that in Euripides' extensive development of the theme of mourning in one tragedy after another, "always" is a prominent theme, as if the tragic genre never ceased to explore the incantatory, redoubtable power of "*aei.*"

I have already mentioned Andromache's meditation on the pleasure women take in endlessly repeated expressions of grief. A list of all the female expressions of what I could call the conquest of eternity through mourning for their sons or brothers would indeed be a long one. Consider, for example, the following list, woefully brief and incomplete: Hecuba's desire to sway forever to the bewitching rhythm of the "elegy of always" of her own tears; the songs mixed with tears that the mourning mothers who comprise the chorus of *The Suppliant Women* promise will always accompany their mourning gestures, even though, as they note, Apollo does not make this music his own; Electra's determination to shout aloud the cry, the sobbing song of Hades that, always, every day, accompanies her father in the underworld; and finally, the nostalgia of the chorus of *Iphigenia in Tauris* that is compared to that of the halcyon bird weeping for its mate in its songs and whose cry is like a lamentation (*thrēnos*).[33] In each case, *aei* punctuates the unbreakable attachment of the weeper to her own tears.

The adverb *aei* seems, however, to find its twin in the interjection *aiai*, in which grief seems to be expressed in perfect immediacy without the mediation of articulated speech. To be sure, the adverb and the interjection—a naked cry of sorrow, mourning transformed into pure vocal emission—ought to have nothing in common, given the great gap between the levels of language at which the two terms are situated. In fact, while a political use of *aei* does exist, as we have seen, there certainly is no such use of *aiai*. The only use made of it in the *Constitution of Athens,* for example, figures in a banquet song celebrating the defeat of Leipsydrion,[34] in which the aristocrats, brought together by the Alcmeonides, were beaten by the army of the Pisistratides. Such a mutually distressing reminder of the past was possible only in the semi-private congeniality of the banquet hall, and on the basis of trust among friends (*hetairoi*) who share common values,[35] for, as the proverb says, "among friends, everything is mutual."

Between *aei* and *aiai,* then, there is no connection except contiguity—contextual contiguity, in the expression of a sorrow that prolongs and feeds on itself, and indeed sonorous contiguity, since *aei* can also take the form of *aiei,* by which the adverb approaches the interjection phonetically. In fact, there are numerous expressions of mourning where *aei* seems to summon up *aiai*. One example occurs in Sophocles' *Electra,* when, after evoking, in the mode of *aien* "always," the unhappy nightingale which suits her frame of mind, Electra addresses Niobe:

For me it is she who mourns who suits my mood, she who mourns Itys,
    always Itys (*a Itun, aien Itun olophuretai*),
Iō, all-suffering Niobe, I regard you as a goddess, you who in your tomb
    of stone, *aiai,* laments!

(Sophocles, *Electra,* 146–152)

Perhaps I should explain this translation which, despite the echo phenomenon that a Greek listener undoubtedly perceived, translates *aien* and not *aiai*. For the moment I shall simply call attention to the different linguistic levels of an adverb of time, perfectly integrated in an articulated statement, and a modulation which is like an index of a metalanguage, a language of lamentation.[36] At this point it is better to emphasize the undecidability attached to this *aiai,* since we are trying to determine in this case the identity of the one who weeps. Which woman is crying *aiai?* Niobe, weeping for her own condition as the petrified weeper? Electra, weeping for Niobe ("you who, *aiai,* weeps") and, by the same token, as Homer remarked about feminine lamentation,[37] for herself, "you who, like me, *aiai,* weeps"? Electra's identification with Niobe is obvious, but the uncertainty about the attribution of *aiai* is so rich in meaning that I will deliberately refrain from deciding. However, my analysis of this passage of Sophocles, so central to my thesis, is not complete until I point out the structural chiasmus through which the chorus replies harshly to Electra's first *aiai* ("leave me to my despair, *aiai*"), with an appeal to reality: "your moaning will not bring your father back and you are unreasonable in your impossible grief, endlessly [*aei*] moaning"). Electra then in turn takes up the "always," for which she is reproached by the chorus, and evokes in succession the nightingale, associated with *aien*, and Niobe, identified with the *aiai* of the lamentation.[38]

At times, *aiōn*, in order to echo *aiai*, substitutes for *aei*, as in the passage in *Oedipus at Colonus* in which Ismene is lamenting her fate after Oedipus's death, or the weeping of the chorus in *Helen* over the sad destiny of the woman named Helen (*aiai aiai / ō daimonos polustonou / moiras te sas, gunai. / Aiōn dusaiōn / tis elakhen . . .*).[39] At another point, *aei* is said once, then repeated in the form of *aien*, now caught between the cry *aiai* and the substantive *aiagma*, derived from *aiai* and which is its pure adaptation in the universe of articulated language.[40] Finally, one might expect an *aei* in a general statement from *Choephori* since it is about the instability of mortals' lives, but an *aiai* has taken its place. Again, a *stasimon* of the *Orestes* devoted to the Erinyes, those powers of the *aei*, opens with an *aiai*, presumably drawn by the tears and the moans which accompany these "benevolent ones with the dark skin."[41]

In fact, from Aeschylus to Euripides and from *The Persians* and *Choephori* to *Alcestis, Heracles, Helen*, or *Iphigenia in Tauris*,[42] the tragic genre assigns *aiai* to the expression of lamentation. However, although Euripidean tragedy is particularly careful to insert this interjection in moments of high lyric density,[43] *The Trojan Women*, in which *aiai* occurs a total of twelve times and is expressed with increased emphasis in passages of intense emotion,[44] is probably the play that shows the greatest concentration of examples of this modulated weeping. We are reminded of the way Sartre censored the oratorio in his adaptation of *The Trojan Women* in order to heighten the political drama. It is certainly no accident that he removed Euripides' final dialogue between the chorus and Hecuba, a dialogue in which, to the pleas of the citizens ("Scream, mother" [*TW* 1226]), Hecuba responds "*aiai*." Two examples of the use of *aiai* from Sophocles illustrate this point.

The first is the famous example of Ajax. When he recognizes the shame into which he has fallen, though still reluctant to moan like a woman,[45] the virile hero simultaneously discovers the sob *aiai* and his own despair;[46] but it is *aiai* (alas!) that he now hears, over and over again, in the sound of his own name *Aias* (Ajax). Moreover, when he allows himself two or three *aiai* (*nun gar paresti kai dìs aiazein emoi / kai tris*), he is also wishing to repeat his own name endlessly simply by moaning (*aiazein*),[47] as avid in grief as the Ajax (*Aias*) that he is, ready to repeat the sonorities of his misery in the way he knows so well, in *aei*. In tragedy, as we know, *nomen omen,* a name is an omen, and to cry *aiai (aiazein)* after the death of the hero, as Tecmessa does, is another way of evoking the one whose name is like a cry of mourning, the one whom the chorus of sailors calls "Ajax with the mournful name" (*dusōnumos Aias,* 914).

My second example is Creon, who, in his confrontation with Antigone, earns a reputation for being everything but a tragic hero. The end of the *Antigone* is for the most part about Creon because the death of all the other protagonists has left him alone, and because he is in the depths of despair. Antigone, condemned by Creon for burying her brother Polynices, commits suicide, and Haemon, unable to bear the suicide of his fiancée, also dies.[48] At the end it is a lyrical Creon whom we see as a grieving father carrying the body of his son Haemon. In this scene Creon's lamentation is endless—*aiai aiai* for his dead son, *aiai* and twice more *aiai aiai* over the dead woman ("the unfortunate woman has fallen dead from another blow"), and finally an *aiai* over the double catastrophe that destroyed his life,[49] before falling silent once and for all.

I could easily see the interjection *aiai* as an indicator of the tragic since it follows the meanderings of the action and marks its stages; because, at every turning point in a tragedy, it shifts, changing its voice as the tragic element touches different characters. Thus, in Sophocles' *Electra,* the dying Clytemnestra takes up the cry that Electra no longer has any reason to utter.[50] Thus, in the *Hippolytus, aiai,* moving here and there among the chorus, goes from Phaedre to Theseus, then to the unjustly accused and already dying Hippolytus,[51] and, in the *Hecuba,* the distressing cry that the old queen of Troy and the chorus of Trojan women had been sharing since the beginning passes in the end to Polymestor—blinded by Hecuba to avenge the death of her son, Polydorus—in a single movement which constitutes a real coup de théâtre.[52]

The Sound of the Cry

Finally, we have come to the heart of the matter. If *aiai* is the cry for all cries, materialized into a generic vocal emission, and condensing in itself the entire register of expressions of sorrow, we may have to look to phonology at least as much as to semantics for the theoretical tools that would enable us to look more closely at *aiai*, and lend it a more discriminating ear. Then perhaps one might really be able to measure what takes place in the shift from *aei* to *aiai*, in other words, in the substitution of the interjection for the adverb. But I am not a phonologist, and so must content myself with the empirical resources of listening. We can at least agree that, in attuning the ear to the echoes in the text that this condensation of lamentation awakens, we are far—I could say far beyond or far above, but not far beneath—from the limpid perception that political discourse requires, where meaning takes precedence over sound. For looking into *aiai* introduces us to a world in which there is no meaning other than sound itself. Let us try to penetrate this realm that tragedy borrows from the very thing which, forbidden any public expression by civic legislation on mourning, is forced to remain shut away in the privacy of the home:[53] the barely articulated lamentation, the cry that book XXIV of *The Iliad* attributes to women in contrast to the elaborated song which is the aede's *thrēnos*.[54]

With *aiai*, everything seems to turn on two vowels, and on the range of their pairings, a, i, ai, ia, aia, iai. Certain words or names thus echo the cry, tirelessly repeated. In *Ajax* we have *aiai, Aias*, and also *ania*, the name for pain, which replies at once to the name of the hero in the form of a moan. We hear Tecmessa's words in my translation that conveys the meaning but not the poetry:

> Ajax, for them, is dead, but to me
> He who is gone leaves pain and weeping.
> (*Ajax*, 972–973)

In the Greek text, we hear *Aias* rhymed with *anias*, reinforced by a caesura and isolated in the middle of the line:

> *Aias gar autois ouket' estin, all' emoi*
> *lipōn anias kai goous dioikhetai.*[55]

In Aeschylus's *Persians*, a long lamentation in an idiom the Greeks considered barbarian, we can follow quite closely the phonetic variations of lamentation and the work done by tragedy in the register of mourning. A small number of words suffices, since to *aiai* and *ania* it is enough to add three more: *aia*, a name for the earth (250, *o Persis aia*); *daios*, which qualifies every enemy as one who tears apart—though in the gestures of mourning it is also the skin that one tears;—and *diaino-*

mai, to "moisten with tears, to weep," and we have the first reaction of the chorus to the messenger's announcement of disaster,

> *Ani' ania kaka neokota*
> *kai dai', aiai, diainesthe, Per-*
> *sai, tod' akhos kluontes.*
> (*The Persians,* 256–258)

One translation of this might be "pains, pains, unprecedented and hostile misfortunes, *aiai,* shed tears, Persians, upon learning of this curse." But from this translation we learn little more than what we have already heard in the sonority of the Greek words, especially if we have agreed to recombine and link words as we hear them: *ani/ania* and *dai/aiai/diainesthe.* A bit further on the chorus again separates and connects *daiois/dusaiane,* from the end of one line to the beginning of another (280–281),[56] before uttering an "*aiai* for the Persian army" (283). And between these two interventions the chorus has named the *aiōn* (262–263) and, evoking the enemy's land, linked *aian* with *daian* (270–271).

Next, we have the exchange between Xerxes and the chorus. I should like to dwell upon *Ga d'aiazei tan eggaian / hēban,* "The earth utters an *aiai* for the youth who inhabited it" (922–923) and, a few lines later, on *Asia* and *gaias* echoing *aiai aiai* (928–929), to which Xerxes responds *Hod' egon, oioi, aiaktos,* "the man that I am, *oioi,* deserves the *aiai*" (931). But I want to examine *ia (ie),* the ritual exclamation which the chorus uses in the evil song of the Mariandynien dirge, characterized as the sound of an equally evil augury that it associates with the tearful cry (*poludakrun iakhan*),[57] and we shall no doubt have to come back to *iē* and *iakha* later.[58] Finally, as *The Persians* comes to an end, with a long *kommos* in which Xerxes is, so to speak, *choregos* or leader of the lamentation,[59] the action picks up speed and the cries intensify. From Xerxes now come only injunctions to weep (*diaine, diaine*), to which the chorus replies *aiai aiai.*[60]

These variations, from semantics to phonology, have led us far from the expressive clarity and mastery of meanings of civic discourse. Fortunately, Aristotle remains watchful, ready to criticize tragic language whenever it falls back for too long a stretch on *xenikon,* a term sometimes translated as "inhabitual," but which I prefer to render as "the effect of strangeness";[61] it characterizes everything in language which is high-sounding rather than clearly intelligible, what we would call well crafted (*saphēs*).[62] Aristotle expressed the heart of the matter, in the very name of this offense against the power of discourse.

The foreigner and foreignness are quite certainly not civic, but, if one were to eliminate every strange or foreign element, *xenikon,* in the tragedies that we know, what would remain of the tragic genre—the antipolitical genre if ever there was one? Indeed, tragedy is imbued with the dilemma of the self and the other. Nothing illustrates this better than the cry uttered in *The Persians.* There we hear the name the chorus gives the Ionians, *Ianon (Iaonōn).* This name of the conquerors resounds, toward the end of the tragedy, like a variation on an interminable lamentation.[63] If we agree that "Ionians" is equivalent to "Athenians" here, how should we interpret this surprising transmutation—carried out in the Athenian theater—of the name of Ionia into a cry of mourning?"

[IV]

THE DILEMMA OF THE SELF AND THE OTHER IN TRAGEDY

In which the reader learns how tragedy, as something other than civic discourse, mocks the obligation to forget and the ban on memory.

> The sharp-eyed courage . . . that craves the frightful as the enemy.
>
> NIETZSCHE, *The Birth of Tragedy*

In Aeschylus's play *The Persians,* the name of the Ionians rang out in the theater of Dionysus like a cry of mourning. In order to understand the reason for this, we must put ourselves in the position of a spectator, because the lamentation will be perceived differently depending upon whether or not vital interests of the public gathered to participate in the Great Dionysia are involved. It so happens that, more than twenty years before *The Persians* was produced, the name of the Ionians really had resounded in the theater as an intensely lugubrious lamentation. Because the city did not like to remember its defeats,[1] a ban on memory had been solemnly proclaimed—undoubtedly the first such ban in Athenian democracy to wrap a chapter of political history in oblivion. Herodotus tells this story in a highly detailed account[2] which, when examined closely, allows us to measure the full extent of the ban on memory.

A Ban on Memory and Its Consequences

Herodotus's story begins with the Sybarites' refusal to extend reciprocity between guests and hosts obligated by bonds of kinship (*malista exeinōthēsan*), the strictest bonds known to the historian. Herodotus describes how, in 494, five years after the Ionian revolt, the Persians captured Miletus and reduced its citizens to slavery, emptying the city of its inhabitants. Seeing the Milesians' suffering (*pathousi tauta*),[3] the Sybarites, who had recently lost their own homeland, nonetheless failed to show reciprocity (*ouk apedosan tēn homoîen*). In other words, they did not, to show solidarity with their hosts, decree collective solemn mourning (*mega penthos*),[4] as the Milesians had done when the Crotonians captured Sybaris. Herodotus does not pass judgment on their insensitivity, leaving that task to the reader, but he contrasts it to what he characterizes as "excessive grief"[5] on the part of the Athenians, manifested most strikingly when Phrynichus's play *The Capture of Miletus* was presented and "the whole theater audience burst into tears. Phrynichus had to pay a fine of a thousand drachmas for reminding them of their own misfortunes and a law was passed against ever again exhibiting that piece" (Herodotus, *The Persian Wars*, VI, 20).

Herodotus is not interested in the ban on memory imposed on Phrynichus's tragedy for its own sake; rather, he saw it as an indication of the Athenians' great suffering in the face of the Ionian disaster. This collective pain would no doubt have been better served by an authentic funeral rite than by a theatrical production.[6] However, the justification given for the measures taken against Phrynichus and his play is of the greatest interest to us, since it recalls the very day when the city of Athens began to restrict the expression of mourning in tragedy.

Phrynichus had made the theater cry—this collective designation was clearly meant to refer to citizens of Athens—by recalling misfortunes (*oikeia kaka*) that presumably affected the entire Ionian family, since, in the logic of Herodotus's account, the Sybarites' lack of respect for the obligations of hospitality is contrasted with the "quite different" attitude of the Athenians (*ouden homoiōs kai Athēnaioi*) based, conversely, on the Ionians' over-valorization of kinship. However, since *oikeion* also designates what concerns an individual personally, we can understand that the Athenians took the capture of Miletus so personally that they could not allow a reenactment (*mimēsis*) of that event to be staged in the theater. This may have been the beginning of a process that would lead them ultimately to discover the necessarily fictional character of any representation.[7] But what they intended to remedy was the scandal caused by the representation of civic mourning then and there.

No doubt Phrynichus learned his lesson; twenty years after this episode, when he presented *The Phoenician Women*, he showed the much more "acceptable" mourning of the barbarians after the victory at

Salamis; and we are told that Themistocles was his *choregos*. Aeschylus, too, learned the lesson and devoted a tragedy to the bitter mourning of the defeated, but once powerful Persians. It appears that the tragic genre as a whole had learned a lesson from the paradigmatic ban on *The Capture of Miletus*.

Oikeia kaka: henceforth, the suffering presented in a tragedy was only that of the tragic characters. These mythic heroes were the embodiment of the distant past, and the Athenian public felt their agony only in a remote way. There are numerous examples: Ajax's *Oikeia pathē,* the sufferings of Ajax himself; *oikeiōn kakon,* the familial, or rather personal grief of Eurydice upon hearing of the death of her son Haemon, among others.[8] We do not need additional examples to imagine that if Athenians could cry in the theater (as Aeschines claims[9]) over the "suffering of heroes,"[10] they could always, like Hamlet, tell themselves

And all for nothing, for Hecuba!
(*Hamlet,* II, ii)

After the ban on *The Capture of Miletus*—up to *The Persians,* and including the treatment of the Theban cycle by Aeschylus, Sophocles, and Euripides—it was as if everything conspired to ensure that the Athenians would no longer risk being implicated in the grief (*penthos*) portrayed in the theater. Not only were the misfortunes described very ancient, but when a tragedy showed myths that were properly Athenian, or those that were resolved in Athens, the ending was usually a "happy" one.[11] Finally, with the exception of the Trojan cycle—an inexhaustible reservoir of dramatic subjects—the myths that tragedy most readily appropriated were about Athens's rivals—Argos, Corinth, Thebes, or Sparta; these were so rich in transgressions and crimes of all sorts that we might say, with the tranquil cynicism of Isocrates, that Athenian tragedians would never run out of material as long as they drew from the distant and scandalous past of other cities![12] Nevertheless, *The Persians* was in some ways an exception.

The Persians, between Civic Education and the Pleasure of Dionysus

When *The Persians* was presented in 472, the Athenian audience received it with enthusiasm and Aeschylus won the prize for tragedy. Was this simply because, from *The Capture of Miletus* to *The Persians*, victory had changed sides and mourning had changed its sign? More than one reader of *The Persians* has said as much, stating that "those events could give rise to a tragedy only if the drama was Persian,"[13] and recalling moments when the play "resounds like a victory song."[14] Thus, when the old men of the chorus listed all the islands that the barbarians had lost and that had fallen under the protection of Athens—Lesbos, Samos, Chios, Paros, and Naxos, as well as Mykonos, Tenos and Andros, Lemnos, Rhodus and Knidus, and Cyprus famous for its cities, "today a cause of groaning" (880–895)—what was for the Persians "the painful list" was "deftly transformed into a catalog of glory for the Athenian spectator."[15]

A *topos* of the official eloquence of funeral orations (*epitaphioi*) states that the lamentations of the defeated enemy are hymns to the virtue of the Athenian citizen-soldiers.[16] Can we say, then, that Aeschylus's tragedy follows the same logic of self-celebration as a funeral oration? Was it joy, above all, that the Athenians felt when they perceived, for example, the chorus of old men evoking "Athens, despised by its enemies,"[17] when the name of the Ionians resounded like a lament, or when the slow march of Xerxes and the chorus toward the palace was punctuated by the staccato cadence of the dirge, *kommos*? Was it joy they heard in the representation of the Persians' grief, where they saw a hymn of praise to Athens? I myself, hastily and somewhat imprudently, have said as much in the past.[18] However, I have since become much less convinced that the interpretation of the tragic effect can ever stem from such simple, or simply ideological, reasons—not to mention the proposition that a tragedy might produce jubilation in the audience.

If the formula of *The Persians* was such a good one, why was it not imitated? Why, after *The Persians*, did tragedians—beginning with Aeschylus himself—turn away from contemporary subjects and demonstrate a strong preference for the time of myths? Historians of ancient Greece argue that after the 460s Athens's chief enemy was no longer barbarian but Greek. Staging the disputes between the Athenian democracy and other Greek cities would have the dangerous consequences of once again putting the *oikeia kaka,* Athens's own misfortunes, at the heart of the theater. Moreover, in crediting the hegemonic city with a kind of panhellenic superego and citing the eloquence of Gorgias ("the trophies won from the barbarians call for hymns of joy, but, for those won from Greeks, funeral songs [*thrēnous*],"[19] said the sophists), they suggest that the new alliance of forces among the Greeks forced the tragic genre to depart from the real time of history and to find its subject matter in the mythic past. This technique proved advantageous because, with the absolute distance granted by the return to origins, the reference to myth permitted attacks that were as pointed as they were subtle.

This approach treats tragedy as entirely political; moreover, it uses the term "political" in the narrowest sense by ascribing to tragedy the edifying qualities of official discourse. By this reasoning, we make no distinction between tragedy and funeral oration, in which men worthy of the name *andres* are found only in Athens, which is thus set apart from the rest of humanity—the "others," in other words the "other Greeks," since the barbarians by now appear to have receded into the furthest reaches of discourse, hardly qualifying as "other."[20]

An analysis of this type is clearly consonant with the civic character of Athens. When applied to a reading of *The Persians,* this strictly political construction has considerable authority, since it clearly resembles that of Aristophanes in *The Frogs.* As we know, however, the comic playwright credits Aeschylus himself with this view of tragedy, a point the tragic poet expresses forcefully in boasting of his play's didactic merits,[21] saying that in his *Persians* he taught the Athenians (and specifically the men of fighting age, the *hēbontes*[22]) "that one must strive without cease—*aei,* the civic *aei,* meaning generation after generation—to vanquish enemies" (*Frogs,* 1027).

I wish to be very clear about this. *The Persians,* because of the nature of the chorus, made up of advisers to the great king (and not, as in Phrynichus's play, of mourning Phoenician women),[23] was probably received by the Athenians in large part as a political play.[24] Moreover, no one can deny, given all the evidence, that tragedy in fifth-century Athens could take on a pedagogical dimension[25] among its other functions. To say otherwise would be to contradict the evidence of Aristophanes, for example, even though with Aristophanes one must always be suspicious of statements that sound unequivocal. Yet the fact that there were Greek critics, and important ones, who limited the aim of tragedy to this single dimension would not in itself compel modern scholars to adopt those unnuanced readings. In the first place, we should almost never believe the Greeks when they say about themselves what they want others, especially posterity, to say about them, and in the second, more important, the tragic genre, in its complexity, is not uni-dimensional. In my view, a *thorough* reading of the text is essential. If we read carefully the lines in *The Frogs* devoted to *The Persians,* for example, we shall have to explain Dionysus's enthusiastic endorsement of Aeschylus's portrayal of his tragedy as a lesson in patriotism:

> Yes . . . I particularly felt joy (*ekharēn*) when I
> heard the *thrēnos* for Darius . . .
> and right away the chorus, clapping their hands,
> shouted: *Iauoi.*
>
> (Aristophanes, *The Frogs*, 1028–1029)

A problem arises right away that does not seem to have bothered the critics, although the scholiasts of *The Frogs* remarked on it.[26] At no time, in the invocation to Darius or elsewhere, does the chorus utter the interjection *Iauoi*. What the old men cry is *ēe ēe, oi oi*, and also *aiai aiai;* earlier, *ēe* had been used in alternation with *oa,* and Xerxes and the chorus leave the stage repeating, and sometimes alternating, cries of *oi, iō, iē, iōa,* and *e.*[27] Are we misled by the manuscripts? Is Dionysus's memory deficient? Is he using a popular interjection, not at all tragic and thus better suited to making the public laugh? Or, could it be that, narcissistically, the god has heard in the cries of the old men (*iauoi*) an echo of bacchic trills, of *evohe?* The latter hypothesis is more interesting, but unverifiable. In the absence of decisive evidence, the question is an open one. Moreover, of greater importance is the fact that Dionysus (who, after all, in the theater was not just anyone) did not react at all the way Aeschylus thought he should, on a strictly civic level, but instead felt joy at the invocation of the dead king by his faithful companions. It remains for us to understand the precise nature of the sentiment that the god expresses. The discrepancy is evident. It can be argued that Dionysus, not being an Athenian citizen, declares that he felt joy upon hearing the *thrēnos* for Darius. As far as one can tell, such joy has nothing to do with what the epic designated as the "pleasure of tears," which relates to the physical pleasure that the afflicted can find in weeping for himself or a loved one. Tragedy does not ignore this aspect of mourning,[28] it is even quite prepared to exploit it, but, borrowing from the example of the epic, tragedy uses it as a theme, as a lamentation within the plot that really cannot in any way characterize the reception of the work by an audience. However, if I am loathe to think that it has anything to do with "the joy one feels at the suffering of others,"[29] it is not out of ethical correctness or for reasons of common sense, as it is for Christian Meier, whose phrase I have borrowed, but because it seems to me that joy is not the specific aim of the tragic genre. Doubtless for Dionysus it is above all a matter of aesthetic pleasure, the pleasure the god of the theater feels when hearing an invocation that is completely successful in terms of dramatic technique, the joy (*khara*)[30] derived from the moving performance of the chorus—or, more elaborate, the shiver of pleasure felt by every listener when the poet has purposefully created a memorable work out of the suffering of others. The key factor remains that the deepest interests of the audience not be touched on too directly by the evocation of mourning, as was the case for the Athenians during the production of *The Capture of Miletus*.[31]

Of course we have no proof that Dionysus's "joy" was purely aesthetic. We are never told that Dionysus, like Odysseus when he heard Demodocus in Phaeacia, wept like a war widow upon hearing the Persian laments. According to Gregory Nagy, the purpose of this Homeric comparison is to universalize Odysseus's mourning, which henceforth is implied in his victims' pain.[32] Yet the *thrēnos* for Darius in *The Persians* is an imposing and impressive moment, but not the pinnacle of grief, as is, in contrast, the final *kommos*. I find it significant that Dionysus's joy—which after all most probably reflected the admiration that overcame Athenian audiences at this point—was not, even in Aristophanes' work, sparked by one of the moments of pathos in which the defeated enemy gives way to lamentation.

In order for us to grasp how *The Persians* was received, I want to venture beyond hypotheses that are better suited to the hearing of a funeral oration. The citizens who gathered in the stands of the theater of Dionysus heard more than a eulogy of Athens in Aeschylus's tragedy. Certainly, the pervasive hatred of the Persians' insistence upon the dishonored name of Athens sounded like a eulogy: the tragic genre never entirely gives up glorifying the democratic city-state, a fact confirmed in Euripides when, in *The Trojan Women*, for example, the women of Troy, who have lost their freedom and are now captives, briefly suspend their profound despair and hatred for the Greeks in order to express the wish to be assigned as slaves to Athens.[33]

We miss any sense of tragedy's specificity if we think that the Athenians heard in *The Persians* only a eulogy for their city. If, however, as I believe, every tragedy deals with the staging of mourning, then we can imagine that the citizens of Athens, invited in their capacity as hearers of a tragedy, to take part in a production of a drama that resembled a long lamentation, were able to respond to the latter in the appropriate manner. In other words, they were able to resist the immediate pleasure of being the cause of the suffering represented on the stage, because, in the cries of the defeated enemy, tragedy taught them to recognize something that touched them above and beyond their identity as Athenians. This proposition seems at first paradoxical in light of the countless examples of self-referential representations of pleasure and pain in archaic Greek poetics. Poetry makes little effort to imagine a listener who, hearing the poet, would forget his own happiness, and in general it prefers to extol the immediate oblivion of grief that the song exercises over the spectator, even one who caught up in deep personal mourning.[34]

Between the Self and the Other, a Delicate Balance

As far as we can tell, after *The Persians* the tragic genre turned away from contemporary events and returned to mythological subjects. To account for this choice, I have previously suggested one reason, a change in the external politics of the city, but there may well be others. It is indeed easy to suppose that by rejecting the dramatization of current events, the Athenians, less likely to confuse politics and theater than Cleon claims,[35] manifested a clear understanding of the total incompatibility between reality, where enemies are enemies, and *fiction,* in which the other becomes surprisingly close. From this perspective, we must insist upon the fundamental relationship of distance and reelaboration that tragedy as a genre maintains with myth.[36]

I suggest, as a way of shedding light on this choice, that we look at the complex identity of tragedy: its obvious pride (as attested by plays from *The Persians* and *Eumenides* to *The Trojan Women* and *Ion*) in being an authentically Athenian genre and, at the same time, the strongly panhellenic[37] character of the public gathering in the theater during the Great Dionysia.[38] Across the multiple forms that ensure its vitality, archaic poetry has always been able to maintain a balance between local determination and panhellenic destination; where tragedy is concerned, however, this equilibrium may well have been destined to break down in a city-state that, after the Persian wars and throughout the fifth century, was increasingly on the road to hegemony, and in a culture that viewed itself with pride as autochthonous, against the background of democracy that both granted Athens exemplary status and made it the target of endless attacks. There is reason to assume that some of the shared underlying convictions of the archaic culture encompassing a system of complex relationships between self[39] and other[40] did not fit easily into fifth-century Athens. Returning to *The Persians,* I would suggest that such convictions could no longer account for the conditions of the reception of a drama in the theater of Dionysus.

My assumption is that the reception of a tragedy such as *The Persians* has to do with a subtle mix of patriotism and compassion, pleasure and pain. However, this mix demanded more distance than a Greek audience—and especially an Athenian audience—could muster; after all, following *The Capture of Miletus*, the city-state was concerned only with the Athenian audience, since its reaction could eventually prove problematic. So, despite the enthusiastic response to *The Persians* (or perhaps even because of this response, which was so exuberant that it could not help but lead tragedy to self-reexamination), tragedians, beginning with Aeschylus, preferred to set their plays at some previously established distance, at a moment between the remote past and current events, instituted by the mythical reference. Once this distance was established, it was once again possible to dramatize on the stage the imperative to honor one's enemy,[41] and, without threatening the identity of the spectators, even to introduce the other as the same. Certainly this was not always achieved without conflict and difficulty, as the plots of Aeschylus's *Suppliant Maidens* and Euripides' *Ion* make abundantly clear.[42] At least here tragedy is back in its element: pain, conflict, revolt, and sometimes resignation.

A few examples of this redefinition in tragedy of the other as the self will serve to illustrate my point regarding pity, the emotion Aristotle put at the center of the tragic effect. Pietro Pucci has pointed out that pity, as the Greeks conceived and experienced it, was anything but comforting, since it always implied sadness and, perhaps, loss.[43] The characters in tragedy always experience pity,[44] but, if we are to believe Aristotle, far from becoming simply a theme, pity was a fundamentally defining characteristic of the spectators' own experience in the theater. Pity obviously is not, and cannot be, a political affect. Thucydides' Cleon mistrusted pity: from the Athenian imperialist perspective, to see the other as one's fellow man was extremely threatening.[45]

The Other Is the Self, and They Are Mortals Equally

Once again tragedy is brought face to face with the funeral oration, the most official of Athenian discourses, and the official mouthpiece of the ideology of the city-state. In part because civic ideology recognized only *andres,* males who were both citizens and soldiers, and in part because those eulogized were dead, in memory forever immobilized in their *andreia* (courage as virility), funeral orations celebrated the only true *andres,* specifically Greeks as opposed to the rest of humanity—*anthrōpoi,* the others. As for barbarians, they were simply that, no more, no less. Nothing could be more alien to this construct than the statement "the other is native," but it is true that the opposition between Athenian *andres* and mere *anthrōpoi* replicates the eminently patriotic opposition between the autochthones of Athens and the citizens of all other city-states, aliens—or, more precisely immigrants, *epēludes*—everywhere, beginning with their own country.[46]

However, taking tragic humanity as our object, it is surprising that the same culture could, during the fifth century B.C.E., produce at least two models so seemingly incompatible. Yet these models coexisted in the daily life of Athenians; or so we must assume unless we wish to suggest that the Athenian identity was essentially a divided one. Returning to *The Persians,* we observe that *andres,* as a term for combatants, can and often does designate Persians as well as Athenians when referring to their military power.[47] Yet from the first announcement of the disaster, and with some delay depending on the speaker and his propensity to nostalgia, or, on the contrary, his sense of reality,[48] the term *andres* quickly yields to the words for man as mortal, *brotos,* and also *thnētos.* These two terms are mentioned in the very first *stasimon* when, almost immediately, grief replaces the initial joy,[49] and they will later replace *andres* in the queen's speech, before culminating in the solemn words spoken by the spirit of Darius.[50] From "hero" (*anēr*) to mortal (*brotos*), the human being is roughly portrayed in *The Persians* as caught in the net of Calamity (*Atē*), because all along his way he encounters the gods. I might add that this portrayal of human life is the same throughout the tragic genre,[51] where occurrences of the term *anthrōpos*[52] are rare indeed.

Is there no such a thing, then, as tragic anthropology? The question is an important one. For the moment, however, I will leave it open and simply observe that in designating man as essentially mortal, tragedy distances itself from the civic "always" (*aei*) conceived by the city-state as a kind of guarantee of immortality, actually the only reliable one. In so doing, the tragic genre seems quite simply to reappropriate a vision of the human proper to lyric poetry.[53] Certainly tragedy, as an antipolitical genre, has a particular rapport with lamentation and mourning.

We are led to similar conclusions by the study of the theme—a lyric theme before it became a tragic one—that life is a shadow. We need only recall Odysseus's words, in *Ajax:* "because I see that all of us who live are nothing but phantoms, or a fleeting shadow."[54] Certainly this is one way of indicating that, like Hesiodic sicknesses, silent and discreet,[55] death inhabits the world of the living;[56] or, rather, that it dwells in man when he believes, like Ajax, in his own immortality, in *aei*.

What interests me is that Odysseus's words—which are both somber and singularly detached, as words are after a catastrophe—are prompted by the spectacle of the transformation of the other. In driving Ajax to madness, Athena (from a point of view that I would describe as purely anthropological if it did not seem to be a strange thing to say about a goddess) intended no doubt to dehumanize him, and in fact, by massacring the flocks of the Achaeans in place of the leaders of the army, the hero has confused the animal and the human. But what Odysseus sees in Ajax is someone other than an adversary.[57] As someone other than himself, does Ajax more easily reveal to Odysseus an image of himself? To Athena who, in a cliché of so-called traditional morality,[58] says that it is sweet to laugh at an enemy,[59] Odysseus, the man of *metis*, responds:

> I am thinking no more of his fate than my own.
>
> (*Ajax*, 124)

We know that immediately after this phrase comes the one about "the shadow that we are." We should also quote the preceding lines, in which Odysseus names the ardent, tormented, demanding sentiment that makes the other, the enemy, the same as oneself:

> I pity him in his misery, though he is my enemy [*dusmenēs*]
> for he is forever bound to an evil fate.
>
> (*Ajax*, 121–123)

This is the sentiment of a spectator since, led by the goddess, Odysseus, in spite of himself, had to watch the spectacle of the annihilated enemy in order finally to declare: "I see [*horo*] that all of us who live are nothing . . . but a fleeting shadow." This enigmatic first scene of *Ajax* may be a tragic apology on the effect of tragedy. Certainly, as Pietro Pucci says, the spectator sitting peacefully in the stands is, like Odysseus in the first scene of *Ajax*, "perfectly immune from the danger"[60] that he nevertheless recognizes as his own. Yet it is a particular feature of theater that we are truly concerned only in terms of fiction. To see the self in the other requires distance: without that distance, the Athenians, caught in the trap of a representation (*mimēsis*) indistinguishable from reality, could mistake the choreutes and actors for authentic

Milesians massacred by the Persians, and the outbreak of mourning would overcome the theater.

The place of mourning is on the stage, not in the city-state. More precisely, it is first and foremost in the *orkhēstra*, when the chorus of a tragedy intones the lyreless song of the *thrēnos*.

[V]

SONG WITHOUT LYRE

In which the reader grasps how tragedy exploits the prohibitions and opposition of political discourse.

> [For a genuine poet], metaphor is not a rhetorical figure
> but a vicarious image that he actually beholds in place of a
> concept.
>
> NIETZSCHE, *The Birth of Tragedy*

The proper place for mourning, as I have said, is not in the city-state but on the stage, specifically, in the *orkhēstra,* when the tragic chorus intones a lamentation, a *thrēnos.*

Does the attempt to ascertain the connection between tragedy as a genre and the observances and portrayals of mourning lead us back to an untimely[1]—unfashionable if not actually forbidden[2]—dispute about the origin of tragedy? I don't think so, despite the fact that the Nietzschean allure—birth rather than origin—of that designation appeals to me. While I see no rationally based obligation to revisit the question of the birth or origin of tragedy,[3] anyone choosing to do so would do well to invent new terms. Once we acknowledge that our age no longer believes in simple causes, we should reject any claim of a pure and simple alternative that aims to situate the birth of tragedy either in the cult of the hero or in that of Dionysus,[4] and instead wager upon an origin that is by definition overdetermined. This is not the time, however, to return to the oldest of questions: for now, contemporary problems are sufficient.

By inviting the reader to listen to the mourning voice in tragedy I wish not only to emphasize listening over seeing in theatrical representation,[5] but also song over discourse (*logos*) and to heed the lyric passages over the iambic meter of dialogue, in other words to focus more on the chorus than on the protagonists. Admittedly this choice, by emphasizing the role of song in tragedy over the evolution of the genre toward ever more discursive forms, appears anti-Aristotelian. In fact, by privileging the role of the song, I am choosing a problematic of origin over one of finality (*telos*). For this reason, I am less interested in Aeschylus as the playwright who reduced the role of the chorus and made discourse the true protagonist,[6] and more in the author of *The Persians, The Suppliant Maidens,* and *Agamemnon,* where the choral parts are so important that one might almost take the chorus to be the protagonist.[7] In short, taking as the object of my study the voice of tragedy means, as Charles Segal has suggested, treating song as an "active" element, powerful enough to pervade the plot. For example, in the *Oresteia,* in the metaphorical fabric of the texts, song even intrudes thematically into iambic—and hence, by definition—"spoken" passages.[8]

This discussion takes us back to the question of the relationship between tragedy and the forms of lyric poetry during the archaic period. The question is controversial, as we have seen: scholars such as John Herrington are convinced that tragedy is heir to the poetic tradition in its entirety,[9] whereas others such as Gregory Nagy argue—supported by certain passages in Plato—that if tragedy made itself heir to the various lyric genres, it did so by dissolving their specific features, making them its own.[10]

The situation is further complicated by the fact that lyric poetry tends to present the various Greek forms of song, which tragedy either incorporates or expels, as foreign to one another, and even as foreign to the shared Greek tradition,[11] beginning with lamentation. Lamentation has a Homeric pedigree, but its origins have been traced to Asia, owing to the many cross-references between the Asiatic sung lament and the ritual mourning song, the Aryan "*kommos*" and the strident accents of the "Cissian wailing woman" (*ielemistria*).[12] Moreover, the tradition insistently holds that the flute, the *aulos,* which by definition accompanies both lamentations and the singing of tragic choruses, is Phrygian by origin.[13] We cannot fail to sense, even more acutely than ever—and in this case embedded in the tragic form itself—the tension between the same and the other so characteristic of the tragic genre.[14] Before ending the list of the many figures of alterity, I might add that Dionysus the Greek, whose existence is now attested as far back as the Mycenean era, was to the Greeks themselves the most "oriental" of foreigners.

We can all agree that there are numerous and striking similarities between tragedy and lamentation.[15] However, how are we to reconcile this with all that has been said about the antipolitical bent of tragedy? If we recall, for example, the repeated efforts of city-states to limit any show of grief, especially when it was thought to introduce into the closed universe of civic life some internal other: women wailing, "barbaric" cries, "oriental" music? Are we to regard tragedy's predilection for evoking grief (*penthos*) as grounds, and eminently political ones, for some claim of autonomy proper to the genre?[16] Or, on the contrary, are we to infer from tragedy's familiarity with *thrēnos,* its more complex ties to civic orthodoxy?

It is always possible to give up the search for a meaning and, like the authors of a work on the funerary practices of the Greeks, say that these ties (between tragedy and *thrēnos*), being of the order of established facts, need no further explanation. If, however, we refuse, as I do, to assert that lamentations, those "highly personal expressions of grief which appear often in the works of the tragedians in a fairly direct and simple form,"[17] need no further comment, how do we deal with the fact that, in order to carry out an analysis that distinguishes between lamentation in the tragic genre and outside of it, one must employ information about *thrēnos* that comes almost exclusively from tragic texts?

In order to break out of this closed circle, is it necessary, conversely, to deny that threnody has any theatrical potential? Support for doing so may be found in Gregory Nagy's reading of a passage from *The Frogs* in which he says that Aristophanes' Aeschylus portrays *thrēnos* as one of the nontheatrical elements that Euripides rashly attaches to tragic drama.[18] However, beside the fact that a critique of "threnody" as tragic material by the author of *The Persians* would undoubtedly be out of place, it is likely that, when he accuses Euripides of borrowing widely (*apo pantōn*) from "prostitutes' songs, *skolia* of Meletos, Carian flutings, dirges (*thrēnoi*), dance hall music" (Aristophanes, *The Frogs,* 1301–1302), Aristophanes-Aeschylus is aiming more at the heterogeneous nature of the mix than at the theatrical or nontheatrical quality of its components.[19] Thus we ought rather to turn to the tragic texts themselves to inquire about what they intended to derive from lamentation and how they used it. We observe once again that, within the spectrum of Athenian forms of discourse, tragedy often holds very unorthodox positions.

Glory, Song, Tears

According to epic, what is heard in lamentation, in *thrēnos,* is the successful union of grief and the promise of immortality, of *penthos* and *kleos.* The epic model of this "praising through tears"[20] (or, as Aeschylus puts it in a striking oxymoron, the moaning of glory)[21] is probably what the Muses themselves, with splendid voices, sing for Achilles.[22] Truly, it was the goddesses, the keepers of song, who celebrated the "best of the Achaeans." Still, this does not enlighten us about the lyric form when performers and addressees were less-exalted individuals.

The next major stage in a rough tracking of the development of *thrēnos* is the city-state. Our concern is to find out what happened at that time in the transition from Homeric lamentation to civic funeral, since *thrēnos,* with its ties to eulogy severed, has now become the perfect foil for political discourse that, in Athens, is the sole keeper and purveyor of memory. Whether we recall Solon's funeral legislation forbidding threnody in verse at funeral ceremonies or the repeated criticism of it in funeral orations (*epitaphios*), the rejection of *thrēnos* is strikingly radical. In the case of funeral orations, at least, *thrēnos,* drained of all specificity (in other words, of any lyric dimension) and apparently deprived of any reference to glory,[23] seems to designate only a kind of "moaning."

The contrast is all the more striking for someone who, relying upon this civic rejection (perhaps we should say Athenian, or even democratic rejection), enters the universe of tragedy, where the mere mention of the word *thrēnos* seems bound to provoke at the very heart of the text a suffering (*pathos*) sufficient to summon up moving echoes of the myriad forms of Greek music.

Of course in tragedy one may occasionally come across a declaration on the vanity of *thrēnos* worthy of a funeral oration or *epitaphios:* "Ah, wretched me. I am blinded, the light has been torn from my eyes!" cries Polymestor in *Hecuba*[24] (Euripides, *Hecuba,* 1035). Admonishing himself not to give in to the temptation to mourn, Ajax declares: "No good is done by futile lamentation."[25] Aeschylus's Kratos (Power), for his part, vehemently addresses Hephaestus who, reluctant to nail Prometheus to his rock, has reproached him as much for his impudence as for his stubbornness:

"For wailing thus will do him no good. Do not wear yourself out in vain."
(Aeschylus, *Prometheus Bound,* 43–44)

Despite beyond everything that separates them, these speakers—they are all men, but seem to have little else in common—reject the values of the tragic universe in one way or another; so the fact that Aeschylus gives them lines that would constitute a *topos* in official discourse suffices

to cast doubt on even an officially sanctioned message. For when tragedy ascribes to Polymestor, Ajax, or Kratos a critique of lamentation, is
it not actually reminding the listener of the necessity of *thrēnos?* Polymestor continues to carry on for a while and then, facing Hecuba, the
woman whom he thinks he has crushed with impunity; speaks to her
from the height of his prosperity as a "friend" of the Greek victors. Ajax
rightly believes that he has lost forever (*aei*) any possibility of maintain-
ing his identity and prefers suicide to an acceptance of suffering. Kratos,
the cynical politician in the service of Zeus, a powerful master whom he
obeys slavishly, is power personified: in this incarnation, which he
claims matter-of-factly without any ideological justification, he deems
any spontaneous manifestation of unprogrammed grief misplaced and
potentially dangerous. And in fact it is not long before Kratos threatens
Hephaestus with Zeus's rage.

Can we assume, on the basis of these very salient examples, that in
tragedy all lamentation, whether it be that of a living person for his own
plight or sheer moaning, goes by the name of *thrēnos,* which then becomes simply a synonym for *goos?* This view has its partisans,[26] and to
understand what is meant by the term threnody, it sometimes seems eas-
iest to translate *thrēnos* simply as "moaning." Such is the case for Sophocles' *Philoctetes, Electra,* and *Antigone,*[27] but also, quite often, for Euripidean tragedy[28] as well, in which an expression such as *aiazein thrēnon*
appears to "negate"[29] or at least to dispel the music by taking threnody
back to the unarticulated *aiai.*

Despite their number, such examples should not obscure all the tragic
uses of *thrēnos* in the strictly institutional and funerary context: in Aeschylus's works,[30] for example, from *The Persians,* in which the chorus's invocation to Darius is called a threnody, to the *Oresteia,* where, in *Choephori,*
the tomb of the dead king will receive the homage that the chorus of the
Agamemnon regretted being unable to offer.[31] A further example is found
in Euripides' *Suppliant Women,* in the passage where Theseus wonders
about the meaning of "the wailing, beating of breasts, and the mourning
for the dead that are heard in the distance?"[32] The tragic concept of lamentation found in these examples cannot be reduced to simple moaning.

There is another reason to argue for prudence in this matter. To say
that, in all other occurrences, *thrēnos* is no different from *goos* is to forget
that equating them changes the identity of the one whom the *thrēnos* addresses as well as the musical nature of the funeral lament and would
constitute a true anomaly.[33] From Cassandra announcing that, for the
last time, she is going to recite her own threnody,[34] to Antigone on the

way to the tomb and Euripides' grieving heroines, the tragic speakers—almost always women, as it happens—use lamentation for their own purposes and on their own behalf. Hence Cassandra or Antigone, Helen or Iphigenia will borrow a song that was ordinarily intended for the dead, a deceased other, and apply it to themselves, the living. This reappropriation is important, even if those who engage in it, unlike the chorus of Aeschylus's *Suppliant Maidens,* are not always brave enough to state:

> *zōsa goois me timo*
> "While I live, I honor myself in my dirge."[35]

In passages like these, which depict threnody as a melodic wailing, it appears impossible to reduce the lamentation to moaning. In almost every case, even if the cry dominates, music, whether it be soft or loud, is evoked at the same time; in most cases, music accompanies these evocations, which are often sung. Consider the following: recurring references to the nightingale, whose very name (*aēdōn*) means the song-bird *par excellence* that "sings her moaning like a threnody";[36] frequent reference to "sung threnody" in Sophocles' tragedies;[37] evocation of the Muse with tears, *thrēnoi,* and lamentation in Euripides' works,[38] as well as the wailing dirge.[39] Beginning with Aeschylus's *Persians,* where the chorus, singing, is goaded to shout "the *ie* of the ill-omened tune of the Mariandynian mourner, the tearful wailing . . ." (*The Persians,* 937–939), all the elements of threnody we have mentioned—cry, tears, wailing, and song—have been combined. Thus we can concur with Charles Segal when he abandons the Homeric distinction between lamentation and moaning and argues that tragedy made weeping itself a sort of song[40] since, in its own music, namely, that of the flute (*aulos*), tragedy hears a weeping voice. Hence what is expressed in these repeated evocations is much more than a simple theme, much more than some *topos* of tragedy; it is a metatheatrical reflection of the genre upon itself, upon its origins and meaning, but also upon the incompatibilities that are inherent in it and that constitute its uniqueness.

An Incompatible Form?

Figuring at the very top of the list of the incompatibilities reviewed by the tragic genre itself, is a god, the god of lyric poetry itself, the *chore-*

gos-god[41] who accompanies his own songs on the lyre, Apollo. The chorus of the *Agamemnon* remarks that it is not in the nature of this god to embrace the *thrēnos*[42] and indeed that any claim of proximity[43] between the god and the sound of mourning is entirely inappropriate; in fact, the old men of Argos who make up the chorus are shocked by the lugubrious nature (*dusphēmousa*) of Cassandra's appeals to the one she calls "my destroyer" (*apollōn emos, Ag.,* 1081). The same point is made in Euripides' *Suppliant Women*, when the mothers who form the chorus and grieve endlessly in sobs and mourning (*aei*) for their fallen sons observe that golden-haired Apollo does not accept their songs.[44]

In addition to Apollo's incompatibility with *thrēnos,* there are others that almost seem to be corollaries of the first. If we were to attempt simply to enumerate them all, these additional incompatibilities might well ultimately qualify tragedy, owing to its very ties to mourning, as profoundly anti-Apollonian. Numerous examples come to mind: the radiant god's distaste for the dark night of Hades, recalled by the chorus in *Seven against Thebes* during the battle of the *kommos* for Oedipus's sons when they describe "the shore where Apollo never sets foot, where there is no sunlight";[45] Apollo's obvious hostility toward the Erinyes, whom he opposes in every way possible in the *Eumenides*;[46] the Apollonian refusal to have women sing praise-songs accompanied by the lyre.[47] None of these rejections can be attributed to chance, given their occurrence in a genre in which Hades, the Erinyes, and women occupy quite a prominent position.

However, tragedy's tendency toward incompatibility with Apollo is most apparent in the area of music. Plato, a major opponent of the tragic genre, comments upon this in the *Republic.* He rejects the *thrēnos,* the modes—both mixolydian and syntonolydian—that are related to it, and the sound of the flute (*aulos*), and he observes that the lawgiver must always prefer "Apollo and the instruments of Apollo to Marsyas and his instruments."[48] There is no doubt that in rejecting threnody, the philosopher meant to reject a type of song that, far from inciting citizens to courageous action is, in itself, like Cassandra's song, "a wound . . . to hear it"[49] because it "bites" its hearer in his very flesh. We should take a moment here to ponder Plato's specific explanation for this rejection. He argues that since song is composed of three elements—words, which we may call the enunciation of meaning, or perhaps discursive speech (*logos*), tune (*harmonia*), and rhythm—discourse must be given absolute priority. This is because there is no fundamental difference between words that are sung and those that are not, and therefore "music and rhythm must accompany speech"[50]—in other words, be subordinate to it.

We are free to consider this a very unmusical definition of song; but there is no escaping the fact that, through the privilege it affords to *logos* as well as by the command to choose the lyre over the *aulos,* it is a very Apollonian definition. As Georges Dumézil has reminded us, it is because the god of music presides primarily over speech, the instrument of communication between mortals, that he chose to accompany himself on the lyre[51] whose sound is heard "before the song, though not at the expense of the word which it merely accompanies."[52] If we add that the paean, the eminently Apollonian form of song, "shines" (*lampei*),[53] in other words that it deserves, like every "luminous" *logos,* the label *lampros,* then we must conclude that when Apollo sings accompanied by his lyre, "it is clear as daylight."[54] The *aulos,* by contrast, which Aristotle describes in one of his *Problems* as mixing better with the lyre than the voice because it bears a greater resemblance to the voice,[55] is constantly accused of blending too perfectly with wailing[56] and, even worse, of unduly dominating song, covering and even obscuring its sonority.[57]

I shall not dwell on the question of whether that was actually the case, leaving it to those more qualified than I am in the area of Greek music to determine what, for example, an Athenian spectator might really have heard in choral passages accompanied by the *aulos.* What concerns me, instead, is how tragedy itself represented its connection to music. Because of its association with Dionysus and madness (*mania*)[58] the *aulos,* with its "heavily groaning" sound or, as Aristophanes says, "the Muse with the heavy groan of flutes"[59]—this instrument (which one contemporary musicologist describes as endowed with "vehement intonations," "a strong and rasping sound," and of a great "emotional intensity"[60]) is supposed to carry away its listener irresistibly, far from the clear perceptions of Apollonian lyric. Sweet or lugubrious, sometimes joyous[61] (though disaster always strikes in those moments of exaltation when the chorus believes it can safely delight in the joy of being a dramatic chorus), the *aulos,* whose Phrygian origin I have already mentioned, is often qualified as barbarian,[62] while the lyre is implicitly presented as the most authentically Greek instrument. This teaches us a great deal about what tragedy, as a genre, thinks about its own foreignness.

This is why I am particularly interested in the repeated references, from Aeschylus to Euripides, to the close and fundamental association that tragedy maintains with *thrēnos*[63] and a *lyre-less music.*[64] Tragedy seems to have experienced a need to reassure itself about what it was by recalling what it denied. The most famous example of this is the chorus's song in the *Agamemnon* on "the *thrēnos* of the Erinyes which, without a lyre, the heart celebrates like a hymn."[65] We should recall other examples as well: the Euripidean variations on the lyre-less lamentation (*alurois elegois*) of Iphigenia or Helen, closely associated, in both cases, with the *aiai* of the lament (*alurois elegois aiai / aiai; aluron elegon / . . . aiagmasi*). Iphigenia delights in stressing the negativity of her dirge (*dusthrēnētois . . . thrēnois*) and the absence of musicality in her song (*tas ouk eumousou / molpas*).[66] If we add to this list the "lyre-less muse" of the Theban Sphinx's fearful song, answered by the mourning voices of mothers and virgins;[67] the evocation by the old men of the chorus in *Oedipus at Colonus* of death "without lyre or chorus";[68] and the futile attempt of the chorus in *The Trachiniae* to elevate the sound of the flute, which in that instance was considered joyful, to a rank rivaling the lyre,[69] we can measure how strongly tragedy viewed its own musicality as falling under a negative sign, as if to reconfirm its own definitive break with earlier forms of lyric poetry considered alien to mourning (which was understood by tragic choruses as being their exclusive domain) and placed under the sign of Apollo.

This formulation may still be too simplistic; by labeling the relationship between tragedy and lyric poetry as negative we fail to grasp the striking richness that characterizes tragedy's conception of the song. Could it be that, despite what anyone says or thinks, in every negative statement there is always a substantial affirmation? In fact, a close examination of what tragedy says and does about the great lyric forms that it appropriates and then transforms invites us to go beyond a simple opposition between positive and negative.

Under the Sign of the Oxymoron

How are we to understand certain developments in Euripidean tragedy that, far from contrasting the flute and the lyre, actually proclaim their contiguity, their congruity even, in a style that the lyric poetry of Sappho and Pindar would not disavow?[70] Twice in *Alcestis* an association is made between the noise of the *aulos* and the sound of the cithara or between "the seven string lyre / that Hermes made on the mountain out of a tortoise"[71] and "lyre-less songs." And there is the untroubled coexistence, in *Helen* or *Iphigenia in Aulis* of the Libyan flute (*lotos*) and the syrinx—Marsyas's instrument, flatly rejected by Plato—with the *phorminx* or "cithara loved by choruses."[72] How can we claim such harmony between musical forms when so many other texts present them as irreconcilably opposed? To answer this question, I believe we must carefully examine the references in tragedy to *humnos* (hymn) and *paian* (paean), two solemn song-forms that tradition has consistently and definitively associated with Apollo.

In fact, in a perfectly orthodox way, tragedy associates hymn and paean with Apollo. Hymns are sung by the maidens of Delos or referred to *poluhumnos theos*, the god celebrated in so many hymns;[73] paeans are endlessly associated with the one often invoked as *Paian*,[74] in simple address or in solemn appeal:

"I call you . . . *iēion* . . . *Paiana*"
(Aeschylus, *Agamemnon*, 146)

Ieie Dalie Paian, "You whom we invoke with the *Ie*, the Delian, *Paian!*"
(Sophocles, *Oedipus the King*, 154)[75]

In these moments of theological and musical orthodoxy, tragedy seems to distinguish carefully between the orders, for example, opposing the *thrēnos* sung over a tomb with a joyful paean, or insisting that the Muse of funeral *thrēnoi* remain separate from paeans because hers is the song of Hades.[76] The respite is short-lived, however: numerous counterexamples come to the fore at once, in *Oedipus the King*, where we underscore the simultaneity (*homou*) of the paean and the moans that rise in one voice toward Oedipus,[77] or in the seemingly pacific but in fact intensely violent means of an oxymoron[78] when the text juxtaposes incompatible elements in a condensed formula. I am especially interested in the oxymoron because this trope of *coincidentia oppositorum* strikes me as the ultimate tragic figure, a point of view confirmed by the sheer number of its occurrences.

There is also the serene Apollonian hymn, accompanied by the sound of the lyre. In order to describe its own association with song, tragedy may describe a hymn as "without lyre," for example in the *stasimon* cited above in *Agamemnon* and in a passage of *Alcestis;* it may dedicate a hymn to the dead, as in *The Persians,* or to gods of the underworld, as in *Choephori*.[79] As for Aeschylus, he chooses to call the Erinys's song a "hymn," made still more lugubrious by the juxtaposition of serenity implied by the name of the song and of "dark" connotations attached to these pitiless goddesses.[80] Euripides does the same thing, making the hymn the prerogative of Hades, or Dionysus.[81] We shall soon see, however, that only Dionysus can preside over all these discordant consonances.

Paeans can be analyzed in a similar way. Is Aeschylus recanting when—after stating that there is no paean for honoring the god *Thanatos* (Death), or that there is no defense against this god (*oude paionizetai*)— he identifies death as the only Savior (*hō thanate paian*)?[82] In every case, from *Seven against Thebes* and *Agamemnon* to *The Trojan Women* and from *Choephori* to *Alcestis*, the paean sounds lugubrious, whether it denotes the music of flutes or is addressed to the dead.[83]

From similar examples found outside tragedy in actual ritual practices, must we deduce a fundamental ambivalence inherent in the paean, since nothing is more like a cry of pain than a cry of joy?[84] In tragedy there is a similar ambiguity attached to *Ie,* which in principle is linked to an invocation to *Paian* but which normally, owing to its linguistic ties to *iēios* and especially *iēlemos,* connotes moments of grief.[85] To clear up this ambiguity, must we suppose that appeals to the blessed divine Savior are made only in moments of distress, in the mode of *ie?* That, because of their crying *Ie Paian,* women in childbirth found their pains called *iēia kamata*[86] and heard, unquestionably, as lamentations or cries?

These are plausible hypotheses, and it is clear that religious historians ought to undertake simultaneous linguistic and anthropological analyses of the festivals in which the same cries express alternately, and sometimes simultaneously, both joy and pain.[87] We should examine the eventual transformation of *ie* from an exclamation, a cry of joy, into a noun[88] designating, according to some scholars, a "choral lamentation";[89] we also need to account for the shout of *eleleu iou iou,* combining joy and pain, that punctuated the Attic festival of the Oschophoria. Plutarch reported that the first element "is the exclamation of eager haste and triumph when singing the paean (*paiōnizontes*), the second of consternation and confusion."[90] No doubt, scholars should also attempt to determine whether, in these "chains of vowels accented by a fixed rhythm,"[91] there is, as Louis Gernet said, "an obligatory" and as it were "institutional expression" of feelings that need to be heard, thus in some way a collective practice on the part of a group that "imposes on its members the discipline of rhythm and an elementary melody,"[92] or whether these codified shouts are first and foremost associated with trances.[93] The study of the nature of tragedy leads to similar questions: as I have said, the exclamation *iē* oscillates in an indeterminable fashion between joy and grief. Pindar himself played on the assonance between the interjection *iē* and forms of the verb *hiēmi*. If we note that Euripides also liked to imagine that *iēlemos,* as a noun meaning lamentation, was derived from this same verb,[94] a crucial verb in poetry when the text is conceived of as song, in other words as a pure vocal emission,[95] is it not the case that in tragedy song exists only in conjunction with lamentation, that song is always measured by the degree of grief?[96]

An even more striking form of the tragic oxymoron occurs when the two most incompatible words for a song are juxtaposed, and in their clashing suggest the music of mourning. The best example of this is the "hymn-*thrēnos*" mentioned twice in *Agamemnon.*[97] There is also the "thrēnos-paean"[98] in *Helen;* this may be a Euripidean variation on a passage in *Seven against Thebes* recalling

> the ill-sounding Furies' hymn,
> and Hades' hateful paean.
> (Aeschylus, *Seven against Thebes,* 869–870)

Tragedy's strategy is finally a peculiar one that emphasizes incompatibilities—I would even say accentuates or dramatizes them, marking them as irreducible—only in order both to exalt and to deny them in the condensed form of an oxymoron. Pindar seemed to have no trouble making a hymn out of the "glorious *thrēnos*" that the Muses sang for Achilles.[99] However, because in threnody tragedy wishes to hear only moaning, the tragic genre consistently separates the *thrēnos* from the hymn. The hearer is expected to enjoy the jarring pleasure of the oxymoron even more when the Erinyes proclaim, in the midst of mourning, that they too have their hymn.

[VI]

DIONYSUS, APOLLO

In which the reader hears, between song and cry, the mourning voice of tragedy that mixes and disturbs civic identities.

> And behold; Apollo could not live without Dionysus! . . .
> Excess revealed itself as truth.
>
> NIETZSCHE, *The Birth of Tragedy*

Khōris hē timē theon,[1] "separate is the honor due to the gods" or "this celebration is separate from the Olympian gods": these words prepare us to hear the mournful account of a catastrophe. This is how the messenger, who would have liked to bear only good news on the joyful day of the king's homecoming to Argus, explains in the *Agamemnon* his reluctance to describe the storm that destroyed part of the Achaean fleet. Is the messenger asserting with this announcement that each god has a cult, separate from the others, or does he mean to suggest that bearing bad news amounts to singing "the Erinyes' paean"[2] loathed by the Olympian gods? In either case, the messenger is talking about incompatibility: the incompatibility between a joyful day (*euphēmon hemar*) of homecoming and the announcement of a disaster which, for a city-state, represents a "public injury," and especially the incompatibility between the joy of giving thanks to the gods and the "mournful face" appropriate to reports of catastrophes. Indeed, the antagonism between Apollo and the Erinyes looms in the background. The messenger resigns himself reluctantly to his task, the supremely tragic task of mixing (*summeixō*) evil with good, the announcement of a safe return and the message of the gods' wrath.[3] This self-reflexive moment in the *Agamemnon,* one of several examples, illustrates the way tragedy, using oxymoron to play on the contradic-

{66}

tions presented by civic discourse, defines its specificity by combining elements usually contrasted in political discourse.

The Muse of Sorrow

How might we define more precisely the image tragedy, as a discursive genre, presents of itself through words, cries, tears, and song? William Bedell Stanford, an ardent advocate of listening to emotion in tragedy and attentive to all pure expression of affect in texts, states that tragedy has always been able to preserve the dominance of articulate words.[4] However, no sooner do we think we know how tragedy portrays itself than the perspective shifts and changes, yielding once again to the strange law that says just the opposite: that in the tragic world all moaning tends to consider itself music.[5]

So, between the song that becomes a crying out and the crying out that is a song,[6] readers of tragedies can become lost, and their confusion may increase when they notice, for example, that when a tragic text evokes the bleak song *ai linos,* the latter is never considered, as one might expect, to have anything to do with actual singing. The chorus of the *Agamemnon* exhorts itself to say *ai linos,* not to sing it, and if, in Sophocles, *ai linos* is merely a crying out for Philoctetes, in Euripides' *Phoenician Women ai linos* is purely and simply a matter of tears; for Antigone the song harks back to the *aiai* of lamentation, actually forming part of its name (*ailinos*).[7] Finally, what are we to make of the numerous occasions in Aeschylus when, in a *stasimon* and thus accompanied by singing, a tragic chorus claims to be simply speaking, as if it were time for *logos?*[8]

Emblematic of these unanswered questions is the figure of the Muses, or rather of the Muse. For as tragedians seem to use the name Muse with greater frequency in the singular we should be careful about interpreting this as a metaphoric usage. While *mousa* may often be translated by "song," I would not go so far as to say that the word *Mousa* is therefore just an ordinary noun, forever cut off from any reference to a divine singer.[9]

Therefore we have a tragic *Mousa,* with the *thrēnos* and the lyre-less song in the background. This is a limited context, but one to which the Muse readily adapts. According to Sappho, *thrēnos* has no place in a poet's house, the poet in this instance designated as a servant of the

Muses (*mousopolos*).[10] We have already observed, however, with reference to the *thrēnos* of Achilles sung by the Muses themselves, that the musician-goddesses, unlike their divine choral master Apollo, are not expected to keep their distance from the celebration of mourning, at least in the epic. The tragic genre found in this example an irresistible opportunity for annexing the Muse to the repetitive evocation of mourning as music. From this standpoint, it is possible to see in Euripides' *Alcestis* a polemical allusion to Sappho in the chorus's announcement that the servants of the Muses (*mousopoloi*) will celebrate the glory of the young woman with the seven-stringed lyre as well as with "lyreless hymns."[11] In fact, if there is a reference to a song of good omen in Aeschylus,[12] or in a tragedy like Euripides' *Medea,* whose dominant preoccupation is imagining a Muse of the race of women,[13] there are numerous sinister or simply bleak evocations of the Muse: "lugubrious Muse" of the Erinyes in the *Eumenides,* and, in Euripides, Muse of the *thrēnoi* who sings for the dead in *Iphigenia in Tauris;* the Muse in tears mentioned in a fragment of the *Hypsipyle;* Antigone's moaning "poet" (*mousopolos*) in the *Phoenician Women.*[14] Under the eponymous sign of the Muse all music now belongs to the celebration of mourning.[15]

Still, the fact is not always presented as self-evident. As we know, the *Trojan Women,* the most "lyric" of all Euripides' tragedies,[16] is also the site of the most systematic reflection that the tragic genre provides on the complex relationship connecting and sometimes opposing *Mousa* to the sung expression of lamentation.

This reflection begins as assimilation, with Hecuba's first tirade, once the gods Athena and Poseidon conclude the prologue and leave the stage. Exhorting herself to commence the song of mourning, *kommos,* and to give free rein to her "endless tears" (*aiei dakruōn elegous*), the queen observes that "this too is the music for those who grieve; for them, grief is the refrain replacing the choruses."[17] Thus, with this oxymoronic affirmation, Hecuba, from the outset, goes further in the exploration of the tragic Muse than does her daughter Cassandra who, Bacchante though she is, has not yet forgotten serving Apollo to the point of linking *Mousa* to the evocation of evil. Stating repeatedly that she will keep silent about everything having to do with shame (*ta aiskhra*), the prophetess shouts:

> may the muse never
> make me sing what is shameful.
> (*Trojan Women,* 384–385)

But Cassandra's reticence, decidedly more Apollonian than her Bacchic transports would have led us to expect, does not find the conventional echo in the Trojan women of the chorus, who, weeping for the defeat of Ilium, appeal to the Muse:

> Muse, cry and inspire in me
> A new hymn for Troy, a mourning song.
> For her will resound my cry of mourning.
>
> (511–515)

The chorus evokes the Muse again in order to comment on the painful exchange that opens the meeting between Hecuba and Andromache; this evocation is no longer sufficient in itself since from this point on tears and moaning are what will give meaning to the noun *mousa:*

> What mourning song, what lamentation,
> What flow of tears!
>
> (607–608)

Hecuba has the last word, and when, in that final moment she bends over the broken body of Astyanax and plumbs the depths of despair, we might well credit her with a new variation on the Muse of tears. Euripides' genius is all the more striking when, *in fine,* he unexpectedly has the fallen queen express concern for *kleos* in tones fraught with epic connotations.

> But if a divinity had buried us underground
> We would have disappeared without being sung of,
> Without providing a theme for song to the Muses of poets to come.
>
> (1241–1244)

The words are surprising, and their bitter irony is equaled only by the ambiguity of the message. By substituting glory for lamentation and the Muses for the Muse, Hecuba, in the end, restores to the musician goddesses all their former prerogatives—for the future, though not for the present. However, the future, which exists in the epic as horizon even in performance, has no status in the theater since tragedy knows only the present moment of catastrophe. What, then, is the unthinkable temporality that will restore the Muses to their vocation?

To understand this point, we must look again at the plural form of the term. Occurrences of the plural are rare, and by that token all the more troubling. Leaving aside the "patriotic" annexations of the Muses for the benefit of Athens or Colonus,[18]—obligatory tributes of the tragic genre to its Athenian roots—I must mention two particularly remarkable evocations of the chorus of Muses by tragic choruses.

One speech, a *stasimon* in *Antigone,* offers the first example of one highly unusual form. Antigone has just departed for the last time, celebrating her own piety, and the chorus sings about the requirement of submitting to the gods, or rather—as it is really thinking of only one god—to Dionysus. After a strophe on Danaë, the antistrophe is dedicated to Lycurgus, king of the Edonians, persecutor of Dionysus in the *Antigone* just as he was in *The Iliad.* Lycurgus is punished for offenses against both the fire of the *evohe* and the women possessed by the god (*entheous gunaikas*) as well as against the Muses, lovers of the *aulos.*[19] One scholar reminds us that Dionysus, called in Athens by the title *Melpomenos* (the tragic Muse is called Melpomena, as we know), maintains a close relationship with the Muses.[20] Nevertheless, in view of the poetic tradition common to the Greeks, there is something strange in the evocation of these Dionysian Muses, friends of the *aulos.*

In the same way, the *aulos* dominates Euripides' *Heracles,* from which I take my second example. Heracles, the conquering hero, appears just in time to save his wife and sons from certain death, and the chorus of the old men of Thebes sings its joy at rediscovering the Muses, as if the goddesses had been keeping themselves aloof from the celebration of sorrow. It proclaims:

> I shall not cease mingling
> The Graces and the Muses,
> (*Heracles,* 679–680)

and it adds, though it is imprudent for humans to wager on eternity:[21]

> I could not live without them (Muses),
> Live without their garlands.
> (676–677)

No sooner is the ancient song celebrating Memory, the mother of the Muses, linked to the new song glorifying victorious Heracles, than

Bromios is evoked, to the mingled sounds of the lyre and the *aulos*. Following this, and before singing Apollo's praises, the chorus says:

> I shall not now renounce the Muses
> who allowed me in their chorus (m'ekhoreusan).[22]
>
> (685–686)

We know what becomes of the vows made by the chorus. Raging Madness (*Lyssa*) "will make Heracles dance" like a Bacchante[23] to the sound of the flute, and the messenger will come to announce that Heracles has killed the very ones he had saved, his own wife and sons. Once again, the chorus, in consternation, is definitively committed to celebrating mourning: ("*Aiai,* how shall we find enough tears, enough songs of mourning, hymns for the dead, the choruses of Hades?").[24] But before resigning themselves, and as if to better measure the extent of the catastrophe, the old men of Thebes evoked two mythic precedents: the crime of the Danaides, which the current disaster surpasses, and the story of the nightingale. It is just where we least expect them, in a context of mourning, that we find the Muses. When the chorus says: "A royal son, killed by his mother, Procne. Her only child, sacrificed to the Muses" (1022–1023), we should understand that, in their confusion, the old men of Thebes are ready to find any crime[25] less dreadful than that of Heracles, even Procne's murder of her son Itys which, because it gave birth to the nightingale and its song, has been transformed into a "sacrifice to the Muses."[26] But, as recipients of a sacrifice in the form of a murder, have the Muses not lost the goodwill that traditionally characterized the solid relationship they had with their protégés, the poets?[27]

The Muses were no more able to escape the spiral of mourning that characterizes tragedy than was a singular Muse. These companions of Apollo did indeed come dangerously close to Dionysus, and the very definition of the genre links these holders of song to the god of otherness. Because the Muse came to tragic choruses from Apollonian ones, she could indeed lend her name to the desire for music that, for tragedy, is rooted in mourning. Nevertheless, she remains simply an emblem or paradigm of the drama that the tragic genre stages for its own use. Whether disguised as conflict or figured as incompatibility (Apollo and the *thrēnos,* the Muses and Dionysus, the *aulos* and the lyre, in short Dionysus and Apollo), what the tragedians strove to express was the disconcerting complicity of luminous speech with the alien accents of sung lamentation.

Nietzsche's greatness lay in his ability to understand and write about this. It is still important to truly read this author of *The Birth of Tragedy*, rather than attribute to him a rigidity of thought that comes back to the antagonism between the Apollonian and the Dionysian.

Shared Cries

Apollo, Dionysus. Such a duality is both compelling and disturbing, marked as it is by frequent rejections as well as by hasty endorsements. If, however, we are ultimately persuaded that this duality is an authentic product of tragedy and if—considering the sometimes blatant Dionysian connotations of mourning in tragedy,[28] for example—we find it reasonable to say, on the basis of Heraclitus's often quoted fragment, that "Dionysus and Hades are one and the same,"[29] I believe we have no choice except to return to the question of voice in tragedy. The importance of cries that are also songs, or songs in the form of cries, then becomes apparent.

The first of these cries is Cassandra's *nomoi orthioi*, understood by the chorus of the *Agamemnon* as so many modulations of ill omen:

> the frightful thing in clamors painful to hear
> you modulate, as well as in sharp notes (*homou
> t'orthiois en nomois*).
> (*Agamemnon*, 1152–1153)

Commenting on the shrill appeals (*eporthiazein*) that the prophetess addresses to "an Erinys," the chorus of old men of Argos had already noticed that this speech was not fit to "enlighten" its listener (*ou me phaidrunei logos*). And, as we know, the *nomos anomos*—Cassandra's "measures without measure"—will suggest to the chorus a comparison between the cries of the prophetess and the song of the nightingale.[30] Finally, the word *orthios* in Aeschylus and Sophocles is used more than once to refer to mourning cries.[31] In the *Iliad*, the adjective is first used to describe the frightening cry of Eris in battle.[32]

The reflections that the Greeks devoted to the *nomos orthios*, the high-pitched song mentioned in one of Aristotle's *Problems*,[33] shed some light on the meaning of this modifier. When we observe, in *Choephori*, that Apollo twice communicated his frightening prophecies to Orestes in this shrill register,[34] or that, according to Plutarch, the most authentically Apollonian music, characterized as "straight" music (*mousikan orthan*), was not at all pleasing (*hēdeian*) to the ear,[35] we have reason to wonder about Apollo's presence in this realm of music where song and cry meet. We should no doubt apply the distinction operating in the Greek language between *orthos*, which is often used in a "figurative and moral sense," and *orthios*, which has come to designate the cry that hits the high notes;[36] thus, when it is *orthē*, only Apollo's music should be called straight. We may note, however, that in Sappho, the god Paean who plays the lyre is also the one whom men celebrate with a song—or a cry—that is as piercing as it is pleasant[37] and if we recall that Plutarch was careful to specify that this straight music is alien to the pleasure of the ear,[38] we can begin to understand the dismayed considerations of the chorus confronting Cassandra. It appears that Apollo is never far from the trembling cries of grief.

Still another designation of the cry is *iakkhē* (or, in Sappho, *iakkhos*, the name of the song to Apollo), and the related verb *iakkho*. With *iakkhē*, we are on the side of Dionysus, whose mystical name in the Eleusinian Mysteries is *Iakkhos*, evoked specifically in a Dionysian *stasimon* in *Antigone*.[39] Whether or not *Iakkhos*, as an "enthusiastic cry" personified in a god, is actually derived from the verb *iakkho*[40] is not what really concerns me here, although it is worth noting that on numerous occasions *iakkhē* and *iakkho* are associated with the sung cry of lamentation.[41] It is more remarkable that Dionysus and Apollo share this ecstatic crying-out, and I should like to examine briefly one *stasimon* from *Heracles* in which the decidedly optimistic chorus believes that if the cry (*iakkhein*) is attributed to Phoibus, the sung lamentation might express happiness. Here we must be cautious, however, for in Euripides *iakkhē* may also be addressed to other gods.[42]

But what can we say about the passage in *Seven against Thebes* where, contrary to the logic of philologists who derive *iakkhos* from *iakkho*, the meter demands that the verb *iakkho* sound forth like a derivative of the name *Iakkhos* to characterize the paean of death that Polynices shouts before the seventh gate?[43] What can we make of the numerous occurrences in *The Trojan Women* of *Iakkhos* in place of *iakkhē*?[44] All we can do is accept the evidence. In the noun *iakkhē*, in the verb *iakkho*, there is something like an emergence of the Dionysian in the tragic texts evoking the solemnity of the cry of the enthusiast (in the literal sense) or of the mourner.

I suggest that anyone looking for incontestable proof of the frequent exchange between Dionysus and Apollo, heard over and over again in the tragic genre in the register of the voice that sings and cries, should examine the occurrences of *euoi,* the bacchic cry, and its derivations *euazo* and *euasma.* It is not surprising, of course, to find that this interjection and related words figure in a purely Dionysian context, as in the chorus of *Antigone* on Dionysus or in the *Bacchae.*[45] The passages in which, under the sign of *evohe, euoi,* Apollo is in immediate proximity to Dionysus are much more remarkable; this is often the case in Sophocles, for example in a given *stasimon* of *Oedipus the King* or *The Trachiniae.*[46] We can measure the breadth and depth of the exchange when we observe that the name *Paean* or *Paion,* in *The Trachiniae,* for example, and also in Aristophanes' comedies,[47] exemplifies the endless game of indeterminable attribution.[48] Although this phenomenon is well attested in cultic practices, where Dionysus and Apollo are often found partaking of one and the same honor,[49] my research has led me finally to see it as an essentially theatrical phenomenon.[50] We owe the evocation of an "Apollo of the ivy" to a fragment of Aeschylus,[51] and when, in a *stasimon* in *Ajax,* the chorus announces its desire to dance (*khoreusai*), there is no indication as to which of the two gods is most directly responsible for its mood: Dionysus, whom the chorus has just invoked indirectly through the "Nysian dance tunes" played by the god Pan, or Apollo, whom it invokes immediately after expressing the desire to dance.[52]

The key point here is that my study of this chorus and the semantic fabric of texts that reveal, between song and cry, the tragic representation of the mourning voice (or should I say the representation of tragedy as the voice of mourning, a representation inherent to the genre?) has produced a desire to return to what was probably Nietzsche's fundamental intuition about tragedy. This was his call for discrimination "between two main currents in the history of the Greek language, according to whether language imitated the world of image and phenomenon or the world of music," and the powerful notion that, if there is imitation in tragedy, it occurs where language "is strained to its utmost that it may *imitate music.*"[53] For Nietzsche, all this clearly illustrated how "the Dionysian and the Apollonian, in new births ever following and mutually augmenting one another, controlled the Hellenic genius"; fortunately, to calm the discomfort we, as specialists, feign with the exceedingly general character of such a statement, he says that the child of this long combat or this union is "at once Antigone and Cassandra."[54]

Cassandra imposes herself in fact as a necessary and, as it were, emblematic figure of this journey through the tragic configuration of the mingling of voices.

Loxias's Crying Woman and Apollo's Bacchante

In the tragic corpus as we know it, Cassandra makes only two appearances, in *The Agamemnon* and *Trojan Women,* but they are remarkable ones. The two may seem to be very different, but Euripides' Cassandra is actually an interpretation—a reading, we would say today—of Aeschylus's Cassandra. As spectators we are fortunate enough to have two Cassandras who, between them, offer a concise summary of the history of the tragic genre.

I shall begin with the one I call Apollo's crying woman, since this is how she is first revealed to us. In fact, in the most striking of all the scenes in Aeschylus's *Agamemnon,* we participate in the confrontation between two worlds, two universes whose fundamental incompatibility the text dramatizes repeatedly, but which, despite the structural impossibility of any communication between them, nevertheless sustain a lengthy dialogue. This dialogue constitutes one of the most powerful speech acts as well as one of the most theatrical moments of metatheatrical reflection to be found at the heart of any tragedy.

In contrast to Cassandra, Apollo's virgin and the truthful prophetess whom no one ever wanted to hear, there is the chorus, a chorus in the grip of confusion, incapable of taking to heart the Delphic precept to know oneself. There are two reasons for this: first, unlike Sophoclean choruses, so eager to claim their Dionysian lineage, the old men of Argos in this case seem to know nothing about what constitutes them as a chorus. The second, more important, reason is that the prophecies that the chorus of the *Agamemnon* believed belonged to it—the chorus called its song a prophetic flash, and recognized the hymn-*thrēnos* of the Erinyes in it—nevertheless remained uninterpreted for the chorus, a dead letter, perhaps because it lacked the appropriate language for doing so.[55] Under these circumstances, the chorus was obviously not inclined to understand Cassandra.

Hence the question addressed from the beginning to the prophetess: why shudder at the name of Loxias[56] (another name for Apollo)? It is a way of showing an Apollo who rejects the world of death and, at the same time, it suggests the tragic genre's incompatibility with Apollo. However, throughout this scene with the chorus, while Cassandra remains faithful to the Apollonian reference,[57] she nevertheless retains her bleak definition of a dreaded Apollo even though, after shedding the bands of the prophetess, she seems to be more prepared to counter "the gates of Hades" with sunlight.[58] This is undoubtedly a perfect illustration of the tragic strategy that implicitly says who the shining god actually is:[59] the tragedy insists that it is only Cassandra's Apollo, the one she calls "my destroyer," who is identified as a disturbing figure.[60] An irreducible tension invests the figure of this god. Other tensions follow from this one, tensions that juxtapose and intermingle all the modalities of speech, between articulated words and sung outcries, even between *logos* and *phōnē*, while in the background, there is the complex relationship between these multiple forms of utterance and those of sight.

The spectrum of discursive modes was set forth in the preceding scene, in which Cassandra responded with silence to Clytemnestra's pleas that she descend from the victory chariot, where she was standing among the rest of the spoils taken from Troy by Agamemnon. In contrast to the *saphēs logos,* the clear discourse that the chorus grants to Clytemnestra[61] (for once), the Trojan woman's silence testified, if not to her beastliness,[62] at least to her barbarity: are not barbarians defined specifically by their incomprehensible language?[63] The queen then ordered her to "indicate (*phrazein*) at least with her barbarian's hand," in the absence of voice, to express herself with gestures since articulated speech was inaccessible to her.

Observing that the foreign woman needed an "astute interpreter,"[64] the chorus has suggested something else: that Cassandra is like the Pythia at Delphi. In fact, at Delphi, according to cultic tradition, the Pythia is one of Cassandra's sisters; her visions required translation as soon as they were put into words. A college of male interpreters endeavored to translate them into a language that remained veiled, but was at least articulated. Now the chorus, as we have seen, is quite incapable of translating what it cannot even comprehend; thus it is unable to serve as interpreter. Clytemnestra, growing impatient, ignores the chorus's suggestion, and concludes that the foreign woman is mad. Her verdict, which is meant to be final ("she is mad," *mainetai,* v. 1064), underscores the Delphic reference.[65] Does *Phaedrus* not designate the Delphic oracle as the perfect example of mantic madness (*mania*)?[66] From that point on, the stage is set for the unequal dialogue between Cassandra and the chorus.

A long first movement gives to Cassandra a song and to the chorus everyday speech. Overcome by their own singing, the old men of Argos are prophets without prophecy;[67] they must now express themselves in iambic meter, since it is the coryphaeus who speaks, addressing an interlocutor who uses song to express her pain. Cassandra sees the horror and she sings, for want of any other means of revealing (*phrazein*) her unspeakable visions to the old men of the chorus.[68] Is my attempt to make a useful verbal distinction between what I shall call the *visual,* and the chorus's repeated demand for the truly *visible,* totally incomprehensible? The song's exaltation suits Cassandra's visions given the violence with which they appear, but the chorus, apparently convinced that "what is well conceived can be clearly expressed" would like speech it can understand. In absence of such clarity, it grows alarmed.[69]

In a second movement, one that is lyric through and through, the chorus, correctly relating Cassandra's *mania* to her divine possession, wonders about the cries that she utters—the *nomos anomos* of her song, which the chorus compares to that of a nightingale,[70] the *orthioi nomoi* mentioned above, and, one might add, the many interjections that constitute her most characteristic form of expression as well as the one that most threatens her speech with disarticulation.[71]

The third movement is that of the *logos.* Since the old men of the chorus "insistently deny that they can understand"[72] her visions, in which they believe they recognize certain undecipherable enigmas, the prophetess declares that the oracle will make itself clear (*lampros*), which amounts to stating that she is renouncing enigmatic expression: in other words, she is going to speak discursively, entirely in iambic trimeters.[73] Whether or not she attains perfect limpidity is of less concern than the distortion at work here: the practice of discursive speech, the civic language of explanation and instruction, is diverted from the register of meaningful speech since the chorus is no more able to grasp Cassandra's iambic trimeters than it could understand her lyric utterances. It is important, however, that in making herself the interpreter of her own visions she breaks with the model of the Pythia whose prophecies, even those transcribed on tablets,[74] remain enigmatic and in need of decoding. Furthermore, the vision whose description she is trying to communicate is that of the Erinyes in the house, seen as a theatrical chorus (*khoros*), as a baroque Dionysian procession (*komos*)—but a lugubrious one, in which blood replaces wine.[75] Not only is Cassandra the only one in the trilogy to explain the preexisting, purely theatrical factors that make the Erinyes a potential chorus,[76] but this Apollonian character, far from limiting herself to the evocation of a single theatrical genre, explains how the Erinyes, whom we shall see incarnate only in the *Eumenides* (and even there they will be the only ones to claim for themselves the title of Maenades,)[77] belong to Dionysus's sphere of influence.

We could analyze a number of other moments in this scene from the same perspective: the return of inspiration, the destruction of the bands, the advance and then horrified retreat before the palace, Cassandra's final *thrēnos* for herself. I shall quote only a fragment of the conversation between the prophetess and the old men of the chorus who remain to the end sunk in darkness that shields them from anticipatory sight, and who claim no understanding of what is about to happen:

> And yet I know too well the language of Hellas.
> As do the Pythian oracles; yet they are hard to understand.
> (*Agamemnon*, 1254–1255)

In spite of everything, Cassandra is linked to the language of tragedy,[78] but, as the chorus reminds her very plainly, she is also doomed to rave by the god who protects clear speech but expresses himself in signs. Cassandra may now throw off all insignia of her long association with Apollo, but it is the violence of Apollonian inspiration that, penetrating the palace walls, has shown her the invisible ambush of the Erinyes into which Agamemnon falls under the blows of Aegisthus and Clytemnestra. And there, as mere shadows of this vision of the invisible, stand Dionysus and Hades.

Thus we have Aeschylus's Cassandra in the *Agamemnon*. Euripides, for his part, neither ignores his predecessor's Cassandra, nor rejects her, as has too often been said; rather he brings into the light of day what existed in the *Agamemnon* only in the prophetess's hallucinatory visions. Thus the virgin Cassandra is identified, even before she appears on stage, as a young woman possessed by the gods (*entheou korēs*),[79] but the god who possesses her seems to have no name but Dionysus, or at least Bacchus, since she is insistently called a bacchante, or even a maenad.[80] Does this mean, as in Sartre's adaptation and also in the commentaries of certain hellenists,[81] that the term bacchante is only a metaphorical—"poetic," perhaps—way of designating as mad this impassioned Cassandra who brandishes the torch of her marriage to Agamemnon? The text provides abundant evidence that inspired frenzy is not the same thing as a momentary fit of madness. It is a Dionysian and metatheatrical Cassandra, but an Apollonian and transgressive one as well who exhorts herself to dance in a chorus led by Phoibus, in the middle of the *evohe (euan, euoi)*, before becoming the corypheus in order to invite Hecuba to join her in the dance, to the sound of the cry "Hymeneus" and the *iakhai* of the brides.[82] But when the songs of this lyric Cassandra yield, as in Aeschylus, to the *logos* and iambic trimeters, she claims the right to change her tone in full lucidity and not as one awaking from a moment of madness:

> Yes, I am possessed by the god,
> Yet I am not speaking as one inspired (*bakkheumatōn*).
> (*Trojan Women*, 366–367)

We must thus pay tribute to Talthybios who, addressing his master Agamemnon's "fiancée," observes

> Had Apollo not made you rave *(exebakkheuen)* . . . you would pay dearly for your evil words against my generals . . .[83]
>
> (408–409)

He has understood that on this occasion Dionysus serves the cause of the mantic god. Throwing off, as in Aeschylus, the emblematic insignia of her virginal role as "servant of Apollo" (*Apollōnos latrin*), Cassandra says the same thing in the farewell she addresses to them:

> O bands of my beloved god, ornaments of the prophetess, farewell!
> (*agalmat' euia*)
>
> (452–453)

In comparing *The Trojan Women* with *Agamemnon*, we should un-doubtedly take into account the obviously numerous divergences. But this would also amount to enumerating a list of variations within like-ness, as is obvious even from this overly brief outline.

If poetic inspiration, in the cries of the Aeschylian prophetess, was a fire penetrating the body,[84] the priestess's communication with Apollo seems pacified and almost normalized in *The Trojan Women*;[85] the fire has materialized and externalized itself in the marriage torch brandished by the bacchante. As in *Agamemnon*, but also as the logic of her character has demanded ever since the Trojan epic, Cassandra is not believed by those she has chosen to address,[86] even though the lesson that she is un-able to communicate is very different in the two cases. To the old men of Argos, she announces the murder of Agamemnon; to the Trojan women, she explains that Troy's defeat is a victory since it signals the ruin of the Greeks. And if, unlike Aeschylus's Cassandra, prey to her own visions, who sang in order to conjure away the horror, Euripides' Cassandra emphatically refuses to dwell upon the suffering of others,[87] nevertheless, she states with perfect clarity that her union with the king Agamemnon, to whom she is given as part of the spoils, will bring about his death as well as her own. For this, the chorus accuses her of speaking unclearly, echoing unmistakably as they do so another passage:

> How happily you laugh at your own misfortunes,
> and tell of prophecies that your own fate may contradict (*ou saphē*).
> (406–407)[88]

There is no need to prolong unduly this list of the differences within likeness: I shall mention only one additional element, because it is decisive. Bearer of the victory (*nikēphoros*), as only *Dikē* (Justice) was in *Choephori*,[89] Cassandra, although a wife-Erinys in *Agamemnon* ("a wife even more baneful than Helen"), can be an Erinys only for the son of Atreus.[90]

The important point then is that this sequence of characterizations is still—and perpetually—governed by Apollo, or rather Loxias, who gives Cassandra's statements his mark of authority ("If Loxias exists,"[91] she says, although she never doubts his existence). The god of *The Trojan Women* does not succeed in concealing his identity as the tragic Apollo, since he openly makes use of Dionysus and the Erinyes, and inspires in his priestess the nuptial song (*Humenaios*) in which we should be able to hear the mourning song (*ailinos*).

Throughout this exploration of the interplay of divine patronage surrounding Cassandra, it is still the song without lyre that the most lyric moments have made audible. In Aeschylus, the *threnos* of Apollo's bacchante states that soon her prophetic song would have a place only on the banks of the Acheron and would be echoed only in the Cocytus (*Kōkutos*),[92] the river whose name is lamentation.[93]

CONCLUSION:
FROM CITIZEN TO SPECTATOR

In which the reader sees that, in the theater on the Pnyx, the spectator discovers through catharsis that he is a mortal first, a citizen second.

> In song and in dance man expresses himself as a member of
> a higher community; he has forgotten how to walk and
> speak and is on the way toward flying into the air,
> dancing. . . . He is no longer an artist, he has become a
> work of art.
>
> NIETZSCHE, The Birth of Tragedy

I have now come to the end of this study, in which my sole aim has been to make the tragic voice of mourning audible, a voice not usually heard when tragedy is narrowly defined as a political genre. I wished to show that the relationship between voice and discourse, *phōnē* and *logos,* as the Greeks thought of it, is more one of contrast than of congruity. It is not easy to conclude, however, because so many of the difficult and important questions I have ventured to raise must be left open.

This work had its origins in the conviction that there is one accepted fact that no general study of the tragic genre can afford to neglect, which is that tragedy is a genre in conflict. The conflict in question is not between themes or contents[1] but rather between the very elements constituting tragedy as a theatrical form and as discourse endowed with meaning.

In order to understand the tragic genre, one must pay special attention to the articulation of dialogue and lyric passages. When looked at from this angle, everything becomes important: the different kinds of meter; discordance and complementarity between what is in a discursive mode (dialogue and narrative) and what results from the coupling of dance and song; the more or less balanced articulation between "heroes" (those whom Aristotle called "agents," *hoi drontes*) and the collective performance of the chorus; the simultaneous presence of marked political reference and of the staging of behaviors that can be described as antipolitical; above all, perhaps underlying all these odd pairs, there is the connection, at once conflictual and constitutive, between *logos* and *phōnē*. Conflict, let me emphasize, rather than coexistence. I choose this term not to stress yet again the capital importance I attach to Nietzsche's thinking on the subject of tragedy but to point to the most developed definition of conflict as the creative process *par excellence* ever produced by a Greek. I am referring of course to Heraclitus, for whom, as we know, conflict is universal, struggle (*eris*) is inseparable from justice (*dikē*), and discord is the rule (*dikē eris*).[2] Conflict leads to unity more surely and more solidly than any process of consensus.[3]

Because the notion of conflict makes us uneasy, however, we are more likely to exhibit the terror or mistrust it creates in us than the expectation that it may create; as a result, we have great difficulty thinking of a conflict as capable of producing something strong, whole, and, as it were, indivisible. Thus, in order to avoid conflict we generally choose one side over another, and I myself am no exception. In order to show that every purely political reading of tragedy is reductive, I am afraid that I may at times have given the impression that I am merely substituting what is generally called an antipolitical reading for a political one. It may seem that I am simply reducing tragedy to the staging of mourning, just as Clytemnestra seals herself off in a univocal view of language when she suspects that Cassandra is ignorant of the use of speech (*logos*), because her voice (*phōnē*) is foreign.[4] The task that remains to me, then, is to outline an authentically conflictual reading of tragedy, one that upholds both poles at the same time: the politics that prescribes forgetting and the mourning that regenerates memory.

Ideally, one ought to be able simultaneously to grasp and conceptualize the civic reference and the element in tragedy that resists the city-state's stranglehold. We know that an opposition of this sort is played out between Odysseus and Ajax; between the political "never," *aei,* and the timeless "always" of mourning that seeks to perpetuate itself and that is reinforced by the crying out of lamentation, the *aiai;*[5] between rhetorical argumentation and the songs of the chorus, *logos* and *phōnē;* between the two adversarial figures, Antigone and Creon. Hölderlin, protesting that "it is at the price of excess that balance is maintained,"[6] was able to see that, in action, balance was preserved.

Uphold the two poles: here is the single overriding imperative that must not be compromised. If, for example, it is a mistake to subordinate everything in tragedy to the dramatization of mourning or to the vocal register, it is equally mistaken, in my opinion, to say—even if the intent is to be provocative—that there is "nothing intrinsically Dionysian" in Greek tragedy.[7] Indeed, it is always preferable to try to understand a little more rather than a little less, and though, by choosing to emphasize the chorus or the effect of foreignness, I have at times in these pages taken a non-Aristotelian stance, I know how foolish it would be to ignore what Aristotle has to say about tragedy.

There are questions that we cannot entirely silence due to the power of the tradition that has established itself between the texts and ourselves. Just as the issue of what to make of Dionysus has been raised,[8] in the same way we have to ask what to make of Aristotelian purgation, the overly famous *katharsis.* The question becomes particularly relevant if we focus on the theatrical dimension of tragedy, in other words on the reality and the efficacy of its reception by the audience. It is a question we have already raised with respect to the place of pity in the hearing of tragedy,[9] and one that leads to a reformulation of the problem of purgation—focusing not so much on its theoretical dimension[10] as on the practical attitudes that it generates.[11]

The Play of Emotions

In *The Persians,* the dirge sung by the old men of Susa for the spirit of Darius prompts the dead king to respond to the piercing "cries that summon the spirits of the dead," *psukhagōgois goois.*[12] This expression obviously refers to the sobbing of the chorus, which succeeded in leading the soul of the dead back to the light of the living. The rich legacy of the psychagogic theme[13] prompts me to extrapolate from the action to the *theatron* and from the efficacy—inherent in the drama—of the chorus's sobbing to the effect produced on the audience at the Great Dionysia by the multiple forms of the *thrēnos* in tragedy.[14] Thus, I shall have to imagine the spectator's reaction to the portrayal of emotion rather than construct a theory of the effects of the action in accordance with Aristotle's principles. In other words, the force of suffering (*pathos*) is of greater interest here than the power of action (drama).

The lyric dimension of lamentation necessarily leads to an examination of Greek reflections (including the views Aristotle develops in book

VIII of *Politics*)[15] on the ethical and emotional effects of music. To take just one example, we know that, for Plato, "education in music is most sovereign" (*kuriōtatē*) because rhythm and harmony "find their way to the inmost soul";[16] however, he outlaws the forms of lamentation, *thrēnodeis,* from the city-state.[17] Similarly, the sound of the flute (*aulos*) was believed to have had an effect on the public that Aristotle saw as having less to do with instruction or morality than with *katharsis* (the meaning of that word being otherwise undefined).[18] This type of reflection appears to have been widespread.[19] Aristotle gives it a basic expression in one of his *Problems,*[20] in which he asks "why, alone of all the senses, hearing has a moral aspect (*ethos*) since song, even without *logos,* affects character."[21] Thus we need to speak about emotion, the emotion that forces us to hear the mourning voice.

What might have been the effect on the theater audience of a song of mourning, a *kommos,* such as the one in *Choephori* or *The Trojan Women*? What did the audience feel upon hearing Cassandra's *thrēnos* for herself or, in Sophocles' tragedy, the one that Electra sang endlessly for her father—or for her own lost life? What emotions might have been provoked by Antigone's final explosion of grief—an outburst from one who, until that time, had shown little emotion regarding her own fate? How did the Athenian spectator react to the mourning songs of Euripides' heroines or of his female choruses? The issue of tragic emotion invites us to raise questions such as these; it draws our attention to the way the public received the genre, and it rightly breaks with overly literal or circumstantial readings of tragedy. But we must beware of a number of pitfalls.

To begin with the most obvious, there is reason to doubt that the lamentations of female characters, seen from the perspective of their effect on the public, belong to a single category, one concerned in general with this search for variation in affect that W. B. Stanford calls "emotional peripeteia (act of pacing)"[22] and that Diego Lanza, careful to define the "tonality of listening" in tragedy,[23] characterizes as an alternation between increasing anxiety and its relief.[24] Such categories are, however, too broad and general to be very useful.

So Cassandra, after singing her cries of horror throughout a very long scene, chants her own *thrēnos;* but her song is not a true *thrēnos,* since, after imploring the rays of the sun one last time, Priam's daughter devotes her last words to a reflection on the pity that human destiny inspires in her.[25] Given the calm way in which she expresses herself, it might be argued that this final intervention will bring, *in extremis,* a measure of peace, after the lyrical outbursts that dismayed the chorus and left the audience holding its breath. But the respite is short-lived: it lasts about eleven lines, just time for a brief choral interlude before the resounding cries that announce Agamemnon's murder. The spectator, who has just begun to breathe again, is wrenched back to the acute intensity of tone that relentlessly characterizes *The Agamemnon*.[26]

As for Antigone's explosive lament, the analysis will vary depending upon whether one considers it completely unprecedented or asserts on the contrary its logical coherence at the moment of the journey "between two deaths" that is carried out by Oedipus's daughter.[27] It would be a misreading of the text to focus solely on the heroine's lamentation in this case, whereas the real drama is being played out between Antigone's grief and the chorus's sometimes benevolent, sometimes sarcastic, but always severe commentaries,[28] since by definition a theater audience, during an initial performance at any rate, is unable to make choices in what it hears as the play unfolds.

As for the extended *thrēnos* in Sophocles' *Electra,* a variation on the *aei* of eternal mourning,[29] there is no doubt that the audience did receive these lamentations in a state of anxiety, the way people react to every prolonged refusal to forget; but what is at stake here deals more with the elemental affects of the psyche, prey to a memory that for each of us is made in part of what has been forgotten,[30] than with the simple register of emotion. As for the melodious sung lamentations of Euripides' heroines or female choruses, everything suggests that by repeating the formula from one tragedy to another, the playwright was sure of satisfying the taste of his audience, for these monodies may have encouraged the spectators' penchant for melancholy fed by repetition.[31]

Will this analysis be accused of allowing room, little by little, for overly psychological categories? That is a risk in any problematic centered on the emotions. Some may think that emotion and tragic suffering (*pathos* and *pathema*)[32] differ by their very nature, and that it would be a mistake to confuse the reaction to a theatrical "passion" with any individual feelings. We need, therefore, to focus on those elements of tragedy that refer to social practices familiar to the audience.

The Individual, the Collectivity, the Theater

A perfect example is the exhibition of the corpse, which is both a primary feature of tragic representation and "an eminently ritual act." The

display (*prothesis*) of the corpse "[reproducing] a religious practice familiar to the audience," would allow the spectators to recognize a ritualized
reality within the disturbing displacement of the familiar in tragedy.[33] A
similar analysis can be made of the mourning song scenes, which many
scholars view as faithful reproductions of shared social experiences for
the audience. It has thus been suggested that "these acts of funereal
piety, [although] integrated in the dramatic fabric at different levels of
formalization, [. . .] all exercise the same function: that of bringing the
audience back from the disquieting anomaly of tragic violence to the
framework of known and hence reassuring religious practice. By reliev-
ing the paralysis of grief through phonic and mimetic means, lamentation becomes, even in theatrical representation, an element that com-
pensates for afflictions; it corrects emotion through rigorously defined
institutional forms of expression."[34] Let us agree that lamentation, as a
social practice—in his study on lamentation in tragedy, Ernesto De
Martino would call it ritual[35]—relieves suffering and redirects the excess,
to honor a term from Herodotus and Sophocles,[36] toward codified songs
and acts. This normative and reassuring representation of society as a
functional site of all balance is very widely shared. I doubt, however,
that it is relevant to an understanding of the tragic genre. For even if we
were to assume—and this is far from being established—that a social institution could be portrayed on stage without too many modifications
that would affect its meaning,[37] we cannot assume that simply recogniz-
ing it for what it is in everyday life means that it will have the same effect upon the audience. Moreover, we would have to distinguish between the effect that the portrayal of an institution exercises, within the
plot, on the agents of the drama, and the feeling of relief that the audience is supposed to feel—relief at having recognized the familiar, but
also it seems, closely linked to this, the calm that is almost automatically
brought about by the performances of the *kommos,* the funeral song,
even one performed in the theater.

The point is that the theater is about theater. That is precisely, in my
view, the principal objection one can make against such a construct.
Theater is mimesis; no doubt there will be some disagreement about
whether, by that very token, it is imitation or representation; it nevertheless remains something other than the thing itself.[38] Theater in this
case is something other than a real *prothesis* or a real *kommos.*

The latter point seems to me to be conclusive, owing to the possible
effects it may have on our understanding of the tragic genre. In fact, we
can never overemphasize the extent to which the interpretation of the

same practice can be analyzed differently from one tragedy to another. For example, in *Antigone,* what do the exhibition of the corpse of Haemon (Creon's son and Antigone's fiancé) and the *prothesis* of the corpse of Eurydice (Haemon's mother and Creon's wife)—which, for Creon, are tangible images of his loss of control—have in common with the presence on stage of Phaedra's corpse, which, in the eyes of the spectators of *Hippolytus,* lends credibility to the young man's protestations of virtue (which, though legitimate, are irritating in their bloated solemnity)? The same can be said of the *kommos:* what pain is the long lamentation, which forms the essence of the first part of *Choephori,* supposed to relieve? Is it the pain brought on by Agamemnon's death, which the chorus of the preceding tragedy of the *Oresteia* complained it had not been permitted to mourn? An analysis of the plot of the trilogy as a whole argues for this response. But tragedy, I repeat, is theater, and so we must try to imagine (for want of solid evidence, it must be said) what might have been the emotional unity of time for the spectator of a trilogy, for example, whether or not the spectator kept the same emotions from one play to the next. I do not believe that the meaning of the *kommos* we are considering comes down to linking the two tragedies in a process of purgation: for the exceptionally active chorus of *Choephori,* the death chant is the best means of stoking Orestes' desire for revenge for the murder of his father, Agamemnon, killed by his own wife, Clytemnestra. The first of two *kommos* scenes in *The Trojan Women,* where a solitary Hecuba pours out her grief, is less likely to relieve the tension than to create an atmosphere of plaintive mourning that characterizes the human world and differentiates it from the realm of the gods, where bitterness and vengeance dominate. In the second scene, the chorus alone takes up the lamentation for Astyanax. Taken together, these two *kommos* scenes bring catastrophe and mourning to their full realization, before the captive Trojan women abandon forever both their homeland and the *orkhēstra* for Greece.

Moreover, however familiar and well inventoried it may be, I do not believe the ritual of antiphonic lamentation in itself constitutes a pole of civic consensus, during which the community of spectators could peacefully find relief and reassurance. We know how wary civic legislation was of excessive expressions of mourning, especially those initiated by women. The lawmaker Solon is said to have forbidden Athenian women to engage in *thrēnoi.*[39] By emphatically giving a large role to mourning, tragedy lays claim to a logic different from the solely political logic of civic ideology. Although it may be difficult to determine with certainty the nature of this other logic, or to understand how a civic and democratic genre managed to exist in the breach, it is obvious that this was the case. Even if this logic leaves certain questions unanswered, it is no less worthy of our consideration.

How does the Aristotelian notion of *katharsis* fit into this configuration? I believed for a long time—and have even said in print[40]—that tragic representation purged citizens' individual passions; that fear and pity (dangerous emotions for the smooth running of democratic politics),[41] simultaneously released and "purged" in each person by the theatrical effect, found in the precinct of Dionysus a fixed abode with hermetically sealed borders. And Athenians, freed from a never fully tamed individuality, would have left the theater confirmed in their identity as citizens, an identity all the more solid for having been reestablished through the experience of *katharsis.* Today I confess to being much less convinced of the validity of a hypothesis that seems too functionalist and too smug in its conception of tragic education (*paideia*) to be able adequately to explain the complexity of a process like a theatrical performance.

The ideology of the city-state always guarded against the inappropriate expression of individual passion. However, as we have said, the theater of Dionysus is not the Pnyx, and the public is gathered there as spectators and not actors. Like W. B. Stanford, we can always imagine an approach to tragedy that would be less concerned with ways of reducing emotions or getting rid of them than with the modalities to which the genre has recourse in order to stir them up or even nourish them;[42] yet this hypothesis of a spectator whose integrity remains intact, or purified, without any residual passion, without any loss of orthodoxy, does not seem any more viable than Diego Lanza's idea of a *peripeteia* or "movement . . . of psychic to and fro," in which the "recuperation of norms" would finally ease the initial distress.[43]

For anyone seeking to understand the tragic genre, the relevance of Aristotle's concept of purgation is best understood in terms of the spectator as an individual rather than of the public viewed as a collective civic body. In a way, the tiers in the theater isolated more than they united the spectators; *to theatron* did not refer to a collectivity.[44] We must venture such a hypothesis because so many difficulties arise in the attempt to conceptualize the fifth-century Athenian theater audience as a pure collectivity. This new approach, which does not yield to the anachronism of democratic individualism, makes it possible to integrate in a coherent whole a number of factors that would otherwise be contradictory or fragmented. Thus, for example, we know that it was not the Athenians collectively who voted to award prizes for tragedy, but a small number of judges; these judges unquestionably represented the tribes and thus the city-state, but they actually represented it only in the act of voting, since, as in the tribunal, each judge made up his own mind (*gnome*) in solitude.[45] And what are we told about the prohibition of the *Capture of Miletus?*[46] That the entire *theatron* had been overcome with emotion. Phrynicus's tragedy presented on stage a misfortune that we would describe today as "national," thus as collective; and the Athenians reacted on this occasion as one might expect. Let us assume that their reaction to *The Persians* was also a collective one, even if it appears likely that the tragedy succeeded in arousing in them a sense of compassion since the hero of *The Persians* is not Xerxes, nor is it the shade of Darius, but rather the chorus, the Persians taken as a whole. But when tragedy adopted exceptional individuals as protagonists, such as the heroes of mythology or epic, when it staged Cassandra's exaltation, Ajax's suicide, or Heracles' madness, whom was it addressing in this public made up primarily of Athenians? Was it addressing only citizens, exclusive recipients of the performance and of the author's intent, of his "message," as we say today? As I see it, spectators of Greek tragedy were being solicited, whether individually or collectively, less as members of the political body than as members of that entirely apolitical body known as the human race, or, to give it its tragic name, the "race of mortals." Is it not, as we have seen before, the haunting, sometimes silent but often clamorous presence of death that inhabits the tragic universe when man is identified therein as a shadow?[47] If the spectators' experience in the theater implied a sense of belonging to the community of mortals, it may be that that experience abolished the boundaries so carefully drawn in ancient Greece to define the communal and the individual spheres.[48]

The chorus, whose crucial role in tragedy I have been stressing, repeatedly tests these vacillating boundaries. The chorus is often so essential a character, from *Persians* to *Choephori,* that it becomes Aeschylus's true protagonist, one who says "I" as well as "we," sometimes within a single sentence.[49] If we assume, contrary to what some have maintained, that the spectators do not always identify with the chorus, such a vacillation in the expression of identity strongly favors an alternation in the spectator between individual affect, collective response, and a diffuse feeling of another allegiance.

Under the enigmatic figure of this other allegiance, obscurely perceived, I suggest we try to imagine the specifically theatrical experience of being a spectator, understanding the singular indefinite article "a" not as the designation of a singularity but as the expression of a neutral identity. In every spectator the most common reference points fluctuate when the chorus of the *Agamemnon* sings of the anguish that overcomes its soul (*phrēn*). The mind of the old men of Argos[50] is not only an organ of perception: it is the site of the articulation between the external world and interiority. In its confusion, it experiences a kind of self-dispossession, inhabited, as anyone might be, by an alterity that cannot be controlled.

This experience of constitutive alterity, whether Dionysian or not, is what a chorus acknowledges when, speaking in the first person singular, it confides to the audience the joy it feels as a theater chorus, one that dances and says "I want to dance." As it happens, these moments of exaltation, which usually come just before the catastrophe and which unquestionably constitute the most beautiful examples of "emotional *peripeteia*" or of chiaroscuro offset by the dominant note of mourning,[51] are particularly well orchestrated by Sophocles; as we have seen, however, the chorus of *Heracles* is a match for any Sophoclean chorus.

For the present, then, Sophocles shall have the last word, not only because, as we have seen, his art deploys the chorus as the "most flexible instrument for guiding the rhythm of the play . . ." but because Sophocles' Dionysus has, in my view, a strongly asserted theatrical identity.[52]

Choral Catharsis

"When such deeds are held in honour, why should I dance?"[53] says the chorus in *Oedipus the King*. However, the choruses in *Ajax* and in *The Trachiniae*, less reflexive perhaps, or quicker to transform any glimmer of hope into a celebration of their role as the chorus, are more eager to dance, or at least they say as much, and so emphatically that one forgets that they may be merely talking.[54] These are probably the choruses that inspired Nietzsche when he wrote: "In song and in dance man expresses himself as a member of a higher community; he has forgotten how to walk and to speak and is on the way toward flying into the air, dancing."[55] But let us listen to the chorus in *The Trachiniae*: believing against all plausibility that with Heracles' return the tragedy is over, it exclaims: "I rise up[56] in the air and I shall not reject the *aulos*, O ruler of my soul" (*The Trachiniae*, 216–217).

Ultimately, it matters little whether the ruler in question here is the flute, as has generally been supposed,[57] or Dionysus, as I persist in believing for reasons having to do with both the grammar[58] and the structure of the ode, in which, beginning with the very next line, bacchic emulation is invoked with much ivy and cries of *Evoe*. What matters is that, dancing or simply wishing to dance, the chorus celebrates its joy at being a chorus at the very moment when, in the shape of the mute and mysterious Iole—the captive brought back by a triumphant Heracles— grief itself is going to appear (*blepein parest' enarge*).[59] Similarly, in *Ajax*, the chorus of Salaminian sailors, which believes that it can submit freely to the rhythms of the Nysian dances and claims that now it cares only about dancing (*khoreusai*),[60] does not have long to wait before the messenger comes to remind it of brutal reality with the suicide of Ajax, whom the chorus believed safe and sound. How are we to interpret these justly famous moments when exaltation precedes a catastrophe to such an extent that, were we not wary of improperly introducing metaphysics into tragedy, we might believe that the exaltation itself produces the catastrophe? This is usually said to be a way "to emphasize a gap in the high point of tragic emotion."[61] Personally, I see it as a reminder to the spectator that tragedy is theater, which signifies not only the choral pleasure of singing and dancing, but also the staging of a plot.

It is to the great benefit of the public that choruses in tragedy forget that they are tragic choruses. By stressing—beyond theatricality, "metatheatrically" as it were—their joy in dancing to the sound of the flute,[62] as if they were dancers and singers from a time before tragedy engaged in a dithyrambic celebration, mistaking genres, the choruses of *The Trachiniae* and *Ajax* remind the spectator that tragedy is essentially mourning and that this splendid lull in which one would like to believe is, by definition, doomed to introduce its own aftermath, the catastrophe through which, with the advent of the tragedy, everything will fall back into place in the tragic genre.

It is in these intense moments, which are remarkably successful in isolating an element of the representation for the sole purpose of better connoting tragedy as a whole, that the purely theatrical form of *katharsis* is expressed. This *katharsis* is a purification of the spectator's relation to the theater as tragedy.

There is no better illustration of all this than the recitative (*stasimon*) in Sophocles, particularly the chorus's song to the glory of Dionysus in *Antigone* when, having at last convinced Creon to free Antigone and to bury Polynices, it believes, despite evidence to the contrary, in the possibility of a happy ending.[63] Now we know that Creon will carry out both of these acts, but in the opposite order from the one he had announced, thereby setting in motion the drama of his son's suicide followed by that of his wife. The public knows or has guessed what will happen; but the chorus does not know, and the futile hope it nurtures sustains the tragic scansion.

When Creon says "I who imprisoned her (*autos t'edēsa*) shall myself be present to release her! (*eklusomai*),"[64] does the chorus hear an allusion to the tying up (*desis*) and then the unraveling (*lusis*) of the tragic plot? In any case, the chorus sings about Dionysus under many different names: god of the mysteries of Magna Graecia and Eleusis; god of Delphi and Nysa who, like Apollo, watches over the streets of Thebes,[65] his fatherland. From this comes the solemn invocation:

Her [Thebes] above all cities
You honor most
With your mother struck by lightning.

Today, when a violent sickness grips the entire city.
Come with purifying foot over the heights of Parnassus
Or the groaning strait.

Io! Leader of the dance
Of the fire-breathing stars, watches
over nocturnal voices,

child, son of Zeus, appear,
O Lord, with your servants,

The frenzied Thyiads who all night
dance [for] you, the steward Iacchus.
(*Antigone*, 1137–1149)

It is clear that the chorus gives the last word to a cultish and chthonic Dionysus[66] by its final evocation of Iacchus (another name for Bacchus) and his cortege of Thyiad nymphs who, as truly possessed beings, "dance [for] the god."[67] However, to infer, on the basis of this acknowledgment, an interpretation that would make the play subject to the authority of a Dionysus who keeps watch over the eternal life of the initiated[68] seems to me highly improbable,[69] because to do so would downplay the fact that the chorus (which is also in its own way a character[70]), like all heroes, can be mistaken. In this case, it may be mistaken about Dionysus. The one who will appear is neither the steward of Eleusis nor the cosmic choral leader,[71] to whom a solemn appeal has gone out;[72] it is not even a god—at least in principle, since with Dionysus one is never sure—but a dramatic character (a tragic figure, we might say), a messenger who, remarking eloquently on the instability of human life, comes to announce the immense grief that kills hope forever.[73]

The god's "purifying foot"[74] remains open to interpretation. The chorus imagines it marching against the violent "sickness," at once a stain and a contentious divisiveness (*stasis*), that has gripped Thebes. The important point is not whether one should inquire into the supernatural powers of the divine foot,[75] or whether it suffices to see an allusion to its functions as chorus master or master of the trance, or whether one sees this expression as a hypallage through which it is the god—or rather the coming of the god—and not his foot that must be called "purifying" (*katharsios*). All that matters is the surprising echo that one cannot help but hear between the adjective "purifying," applied to the god who presides over the theater—although the chorus seems to have forgotten this fact—and the term that Aristotle later chooses to characterize the tragic effect.

Katharsios, Dionysus? The chorus would like him to purify Thebes of its sickness, but, in his absence, the messenger—his representative—comes to tell a story, one that concludes in a fully authentic tragic purgation. For *katharsis* will be consummated when, over the remains of a famous and unfortunate family, the fallen hero, distraught, cries out the lamentation *aei,* and the spectator, perhaps relieved to observe that all has ended in total catastrophe, hears the chorus explain to Creon that he must leave the future to those he sees before him, that "the present demands action." In other words, the living must bury the dead whose bodies lie exposed.[76]

Today we could call this ending Shakespearean. For now the tragedy has ended. The purgation will take place again, as it does every year, during the festival of Dionysus, on the Pnyx, and not on the Acropolis. Once again, through the evocation of mourning, despite the forgetting prescribed by the city-state, the spectator will be overcome, and purgation will arouse him to transcend his membership in the civic community and to comprehend his even more essential membership in the race of mortals. This has always been the final word sung, not so much to the citizen as to the spectator, by the mourning voice of tragedy.

NOTES

I. Greek Tragedy: Political Drama or Oratorio?

1. I am using the word Herodotus used in *The Histories,* book VI, 21, in which he talks about the effect of "excessive grief" that Phrynichus's production of *The Capture of Miletus* had on an audience of Athenian citizens. On the *theatron,* see Chapter II and, on *The Trojan Women,* see Chapter IV.

2. Euripides, *The Trojan Women,* adaptation by Jean-Paul Sartre (*TW-S,* followed by scene number) preceded by an introduction containing remarks to Bernard Pingaud (Paris: Gallimard, 1965), previously published in *Bref,* the monthly publication of the Théâtre National Populaire in February 1965; Sartre's adaptation also appears as a small volume in the TNP Collection. [Translator's note: Ronald Duncan has published an English version of Jean-Paul Sartre's adaptation of *The Trojan Women* (London: Hamish Hamilton, 1967), including the interview with Bernard Pingaud. I have chosen, however, to translate Sartre's text directly.]

3. In scene ii, Athena responds to Poseidon, who had spoken in scene i about "these Greeks who sacked the city" (*TW-S,* i). Euripides' Athena says simply "the men of Greece who made this expedition and took the city" (*TW* 19). She states: "What I want to do is punish those Greeks" (*TW-S,* ii)—whereas in Euripides she says simply: "the Trojans, whom I hated this short time since" (*TW* 65). Similarly, in scene iii, Menelaus is "the butcher of Troy"—whereas the chorus of Trojan women call him "the scourge of Troy" (*TW* 212).

4. Sartre, scene ix. In Euripides' *Trojan Women,* the chorus refers to the dawn (*TW* 847–848) in the past tense, and as part of a recollection of past alliances between Troy and the gods through the intermediary of Ganymede and Tithon. For Sartre, therefore, to describe the dawn breaking at this moment in the play amounts to a double shift.

5. It is noteworthy that only *offensive* war is condemned and that Cassandra extols the justness of the *defensive* war waged by the Trojans. However, even this limited condemnation of war prompted the idea in antiquity that *The Trojan Women* was a pacifist play (Roger Goossens, *Euripide et Athènes* [Brussels: Palais des Académies, 1962], pp. 524–525).

6. The lines spoken by the god in the prologue are, for the most part, faithful to the original (*TW* 95–97) but moved to the conclusion.

7. Jean-Paul Sartre, *Imagination: A Psychological Critique*, trans. Forrest Williams (Ann Arbor: University of Michigan Press, 1962).

8. Similarly, Electra's speech to Jupiter in *The Flies* (I, iii) began with the startling shout of disgust: "Scum!"

9. Similarly, Cassandra says to Hecuba: "Escort the bride. Oh thrust her strongly on" (*TW* 355–356), which becomes "push me into Agamemnon's arms" (*TW-S*, v). Finally, the discreet allusion to Agamemnon's desire for "Apollo's virgin" (*TW* 252) is emphasized in Sartre: "It's because her virginity can be guaranteed, she being a prophetess, that she's so attractive to his Majesty" (*TW-S*, iv).

10. There are numerous examples in scene v: Cassandra's "Joy! Joy! Tears of joy!" recalls Pascal; "queen of the night" is most likely from Mozart's *Magic Flute;* echoes of Hamlet are heard in "These are only words" and "Words! nothing but words." Lastly, her words "filthy animal" in scene vi clearly allude to Brecht.

11. Compare Talthybios's reply, on the subject of Polyxena in Euripides' *Trojan Women* (v. 270) with the corresponding scene iv in Sartre.

12. Roger Goossens offers a nuanced version of this viewpoint in *Euripide et Athènes*, pp 508–534; he sees in the play a reference to the attack on Melos and a flattering allusion to Sicily intended to conform to Athenian public opinion. Marie Delcourt-Curvers writes, in her introduction to the Pléiade edition: "They will see only the miseries of the Trojan women, all of which adds another charge of excess to the account of Greek guilt" (Euripide, *Tragédies complètes* [Paris: Gallimard, 1988], p. 706).

13. Five hundred thirty-five lines out of a total of 1332 are devoted to lyric passages (as opposed to 329 of 1359 in *Electra* and 300 of 1234 in *The Suppliant Women*). In her *Vie d'Euripide* (Paris: Gallimard, 1930, p. 166), Marie Delcourt-Curvers confirms that the play is a warning. She pictures officers and sailors on the ships of the Athenian fleet humming "the tunes that they heard in *The Trojan Women*. What a musician Euripides is!" She notes further that "the prophecy went unheard."

14. This is all the more significant since, as Diego Lanza notes ("Les temps de l'émotion tragique," *Mêtis* 3 [1988]: 34), Hecuba's speech, which had not previously been sung, becomes a real funeral lament only with the intervention of the chorus, which begins singing a true dirge; the final lyric exchanges between Hecuba and the chorus are thus in themselves of primary importance to the whole enterprise of tragedy.

15. Actually, if Cassandra rushes into the marriage with Agamemnon, it is not because she knows she will die, but because she knows that her death will lead to Agamemnon's. This knowledge is the defining characteristic of her "erotic fascination."

16. As we have noted, it is only offensive war that Cassandra condemns.

17. Jean Prodromidès, the composer of the music for *The Trojan Women,* also composed music for *The Persians*, a "dramatic oratorio" televised on October 31, 1961 (for a review of its reception, see N. Loraux, "Ce que les *perses* ont vraiment appris aux Athéniens," *Epokhè* 3 [1993]).

18. Sartre wrote his adaptation in July–August 1964, at the time of the U.S. escalation of the Vietnam War, and the first production took place right after President Johnson authorized the use of napalm. As for the "third-world" bias, numerous comparisons might be made between Sartre's *Trojan Women* and his 1961 preface to Frantz Fanon's *Wretched of the Earth,* trans. Constance Farrington (New York: Grove Press, 1966).

19. On the role of Greco-Latin culture (especially Greek), see Sartre's preface to Fanon, *The Wretched of the Earth.*

20. Introduction, *TW-S,* p. 2.

21. See Loraux, *"Théâtre grec: tragique?"* an introduction to a volume of the journal *Mêtis* titled *Théâtre grec et tragédie* (1988).

22. This does not mean—to the contrary—that all translation does not have to begin with a word-for-word, close reading of the text, even if this requires starting with an awkward, clumsy transcription.

23. Aristotle, *Poetics,* 1459a 11–13 (in which Aristotle states that words that are used in speaking, or are metaphorical or ornamental, are suitable for heroic poetry) and 1459a 2–4 (on nonstandard words).

24. De Martino, *Morte e pianto rituale nel mondo antico* (Turin: Einaudi, 1958), pp. 205–206.

25. *Thrēnos* (lamentation), *TW* 111, 608; *ialemos, TW* 604, 1304; the hymn, *TW* 126–127, 578; the Muse, *TW* 511–514, 607–608.

26. See Nicole Loraux, *Mothers in Mourning,* trans. Corinne Pache (Ithaca: Cornell University Press, 1998).

II. The Theater of Dionysus Is Not in the Agora

1. See Oddone Longo, "La scena della città. Strutture architettoniche et spazi politici nel teatro greco," in *Scena e spettacolo nell'Antichità* (Florence, 1989), pp. 38–39, and "Teatri e theatra. Spazi teatrali e luoghi politici nella città greca," *Dioniso* (1988): p. 10: here archaeologists are ambivalent about whether to identify a space as theater (*orkhēstra*) or as agora. The best example of this ambivalence is probably the "theater" in Argos, with its three architectural structures atop one another, the oldest of which is composed of rectilinear steps holding approximately two thousand seats, and which archaeologists call the "Pnyx of Argos" (Longo, "Teatri e theatra," pp. 13–14).

2. The reasons for this remain to be explained, though today there are some obvious ones that allow us to acquire a certain distance. This "political" interpretation has taken numerous forms: it is socio-historical in the work of John J. Winkler, Simon Goldhill, W. Robert Connor, and Oddone Longo; it is marked by political history in the work of Christian Meier; it is wholly anthropological in the connection of the text with primary civic institutions, such as sacrifice and the ephebate, in Froma Zeitlin, Jean-Pierre Vernant, and Pierre Vidal-Naquet.

3. This is also true of the heroic cults or cults to fallen heroes, which, by the way, bolsters the "grief theory" of the origins of tragedy.

4. It is interesting to note how spontaneously archaeologists use the metaphor of the theater to describe an ancient agora surrounded by terraced seats; note also that archaeologists suggest that the two settings are interchangeable (see the article by P. Ducrey on Lato in *L'art grec* [K. Papaioannou, ed.]).

5. Were the moves intended simply to find, in one case, a "calmer meeting place" and, in the other, "a safer place," as the guide to the Agora suggests (*The Athenian Agora,* [Athens: American School of Classical Studies, 1976], pp. 23–26)? We may at least wonder whether these were the sole reasons for the two moves, even though, in the case of the theater, the move is thought to have followed an accident, the collapse of the wooden tiers of seats in the Agora, which the new installation sought to avoid by supporting the new tiers on a natural incline.

6. On the unquestionably theatrical quality of the Pnyx, see O. Longo, "La scena della città," p. 24; "Teatri e theatra," p. 12; and "Atene fra polis e territorio. In margine a Tucidide I. 143, 5," *Studi italiani di filologia classica,* 46 (1974): 20–21.

7. I am thinking of the example of ostracism that brought together the city-state of the ten tribes for an assembly of a very particular type; to my knowledge, ostracism has not been studied in depth.

8. For example, the monument to the heroic eponyms, Solon's *axōnes,* which were brought down from the Acropolis to the Agora.

9. See *The Athenian Agora,* p. 91, on the *orkhēstra;* on the performance of the dithyrambs, see Henri Jeanmaire, *Dionysos* (Paris: Payot, 1970), p. 238; on the celebration of the Dionysian festival of the *Lenaea,* cf. *The Athenian Agora,* p. 82.

10. Thucydides, *Histories,* III, 38, 3–7.

11. See Nicole Loraux, "Les mots qui voient," in Claude Reichler, ed., *L'interprétation des textes* (Paris: Minuit, 1989).

12. I have in mind the formula *ou to drasthen pistoteron opsei labontes e to akousthen,* "believing less in what one has seen than in what one has heard" (Thucydides, *Histories,* III, 38, 4).

13. II, 43, 1, *tēn tes poleōs dunamin kath' hēmeran ergōi theōmenous.* Inversely, the Athenians blame the Melians for being spectators *(theasthe)* who "regard what is out of sight, in your eagerness, as already coming to pass" (V, 85–113).

14. These assemblies are an essential part of the argument of those who hold that theater was political through and through. See, for example, O. Longo's "La scena della città," pp. 23–24; "Teatri e theatra," p. 8.

15. See Demosthenes, *Against Midias,* 9: "in that meeting, religious affairs *(peri hieron)* had to be placed on the agenda first, then they heard the prior complaints concerning the festival and the Dionysian contests"; see H. W. Parke, *Festivals of the Athenians* (Ithaca: Cornell University Press, 1977), pp. 135–136, on this assembly and on the festival of the Pandia.

16. See especially Simon Goldhill, "The Great Dionysia and Civic Ideology," *Journal of Hellenic Studies* 107 (1987), as well as W. Robert Connor, "City Dionysia and Athenian Democracy," *Classica et Medievalia* 40 (1989).

17. Epigraphic evidence of such a practice at Samos in the third century B.C.E.; see Jean Pouilloux, *Choix d'inscriptions grecques: Textes, traductions et notes* (Paris, Sociéte d'édition "Les belles lettres," 1960), 21 (foreign judges honored with a gold crown during the tragedy competition of the Dionysia).

18. Aeschines, *Against Ctesiphon,* 32–34, 35, 41–45. I am particularly interested in 46–47, where Aeschines states that a crown received in the theater must still be dedicated to Athena, proof that it is a matter of returning from the outside (an outside) of the city toward the official political sphere and, in 48, where "outside the city" *(exō tes ekklēsias)* is assimilated—clearly by extension—into the sphere of influence of another city.

19. Demosthenes, *On the Crown,* 120.

20. Aristotle, *Athenian Constitution,* 42, 4. Peter John Rhodes, in *Constitution of the Athenians,* offers only a flatly pragmatic explanation, stating that the size of the *orkhēstra* explains this substitution of the theater for the Pnyx. However, the ephebe, in the middle of its rite of passage, would hardly have managed to draw an ordinary assembly of citizens. Moreover, for John Winkler, it was probably appropriate to link the ephebate with tragedy; let us recall that in Sparta, according to Herodotus (VI, 67), the Gymnopaedia took place in the "theater."

21. Simon Goldhill was quite right to observe in "The Great Dionysia and Civic Ideology" (p. 60, n. 16) that in *The Invention of Athens,* I deal with the question of orphans only in terms of the ephebate without taking up the question of the theatrical dimension of the institution; but to deal with the latter question, I think, would also require taking on the relationship of theater to mourning.

22. See Lysias, *Against Theozotides*, 2, and Isocrates, *On Peace*, 83, as well as Aeschines, *Against Ctesiphon*, 153–154.

23. We should probably not, like Simon Goldhill ("The Great Dionysia and Civic Ideology," pp. 63–65), take Aeschines' text on this point too seriously and assume that the ritual had probably disappeared. One could just as well use *Against Theozotides* to say that Theozotides' decree threatened the very existence of the institution.

24. Aeschines, *Against Ctesiphon*, 154, 153.

25. Aristophanes, *The Frogs*, 1053–1055; recall, for example, that in Thucydides this term refers to the age group of men eligible for the service and therefore perfectly qualified to be citizens.

26. Participating in tragic choruses seems to have been an essential component of the life of a citizen, if we are to believe the fragment of Athenian ideology provided by Xenophon in the discourse of Kleocritos (*Hellenica*, II, 4, 20): "We have participated with you in the most solemn ceremonies, at sacrifices and at the most beautiful festivals, we have been *choreutai* together, students and soldiers together. . . ." See also Loraux, *La cité divisée. L'oubli dans la mémoire d'Athènes* (Paris: Payot, 1997).

27. If it is true that the existence of choruses symbolizes peacetime (Aristophanes, *Frogs*, 1419).

28. John Winkler, ("The Ephebes' Song: Tragoidia and Polis," in Winkler and Froma I. Zeitlin, eds., *Nothing to Do with Dionysos? Athenian Drama in Its Social Context* [Princeton: Princeton University Press, 1990], pp. 30–31), as well as Oddone Longo ("Atene," pp. 24–25); one wonders what was done about foreigners. On judges, see Diego Lanza, "Lo spettacolo," in M. Vegetti, ed., *Oralità scrittura spettacolo* (Turin, 1983), p. 111.

29. Goldhill, "The Great Dionysia," p. 60.

30. Peter Euben speaks of "an institution *analogous* to the *eliaia*, to the council (*boulē*) or to the assembly (*ekklēsia*)" (Introduction to *Greek Tragedy and Political Theory* [Berkeley: University of California Press, 1986], p. 22); emphasis added.

31. This is precisely what Athenian orators found scandalous about any event in the theater that was not strictly theatrical: for example, in the fifth century, payment of the tribute in the packed theater (Isocrates, *Peace*, 82), in the fourth century, the emancipation of slaves "with all Greeks as witnesses" (Aeschines, *Against Ctesiphon*, 42).

32. It may also happen, as in the *Choephori* (and this departure is all the more remarkable), that a chorus of slaves dominates the action by taking the initiative repeatedly: see Marsh McCall, "The Chorus of Aeschylus' *Choephori*," in M. Griffith and D. Mastronarde, *Cabinet of the Muses* (Atlanta: Scholars Press, 1990), p. 32. McCall believes that Aeschylus invested this chorus of slaves with "the presence and the aura of . . . citizens" quite deliberately.

33. Preface to Aeschylus, p. 28, preface to Sophocles, pp. 20–21, preface to Baldry, pp. VI-VIII.

34. Preface to Aeschylus, p. 28; preface to Baldry, p. VIII; preface to Sophocles, p. 15 (in which Vidal-Naquet addresses some of the analyses Hannah Arendt presents in *The Human Condition*). These statements are all the more interesting considering that Vidal-Naquet has also been known to state that "Tragedy is politics."

35. *Choephori*, 461.

36.. Sophocles, *Electra*, 88, 94, 103–104, 231, 254–255, 530.

37. On the sanction against the *thrēnos*, see N. Loraux, *The Invention of Athens: The Funeral Oration and the Classical City*, trans. Alan Sheridan (Cambridge: Harvard University Press, 1986), pp. 49–50.

38. *Electra*, 481, *ou gar pot' amnestei;* the chorus in fact attributes the rejection of amnesty to Agamemnon, but Electra claims it as her own.

39. *Electra*, 1227.

40. Another overdetermining reason for this analysis can be cited: Sophocles' reading of *Choephori*, in reaction to the extremely unusual nature of the chorus in Aeschylus (see note 32, above), underscores his strategy of variation within difference by using this surprising term of address.

41. Sophocles, *Electra*, 244–250; see Aeschylus, *Eumenides*, 690–691 (in which Athena repeats the declarations of the Erinyes in 516–524).

42. Baldry clearly saw this point (p. 189).

43. *Electra*, 477, *Dika dikaia pheromena kheroin kratē;* compare this with *Eumenides*, 973–975, *ekratēse / Zeus Agoraios.*

44. Sophocles, *Electra*, 490.

45. Euripides, *Electra*, 1337.

46. If, like Jebb and Lloyd-Jones-Wilson, we accept the correction; but, as Gordon Kirkwood pointed out to me, text of the manuscripts (*oud; ekhō legein*) is perfectly acceptable, in which case the chorus says that "it has nothing to say."

47. Here we are concerned with line 1498, *ta t'onta kai mellonta Pelopidon kaka*, but it is true that the speaker is Aegisthus, which may not deprive his words of all credibility, but might lead the reader to neglect this discrete allusion.

48. Another use of the verb *telein* by the chorus at the time of Clytemnestra's murder in *Electra*, 1419 (*telous' arai*). For a few striking uses of words derived from *telos*, especially *teleios*, see *Agamemnon*, 972–973, 1107, etc.

49. See Loraux, *La cité divisée*.

50. See Aristophanes, *Frogs*, 1419. Dionysus himself explains to Aeschylus and to Euripides that he has come so that the city, being saved, might organize choruses.

51. Xenophon, *Hellenica*, IV, 4, 2–3. See an analogous episode: the Eleans' invasion of Olympus on the day of the games (Xen., *Hell.*, VII, 31), which is described with less indignation because it does not involve *stasis* and because the theater in this case functions only as a spatial indicator (comprising the area bounded by the Bouleuterion, the sanctuary of Hestia and the adjacent theater).

52. A murder which, to a Greek, is the ultimate horror (see Loraux, *La cité divisée*).

53. Thucydides, III, 81, 5.

54. Lysias, *Against Agoratus*, 32.

55. See the commentary of Louis Gernet on a passage from *Against Agoratos*: Gernet aptly quotes Thucydides, VIII, 67, 2, in which the verb *xunekleisan* rightly signifies that the assembly was "piled up" in too small a space.

56. Thucydides, VIII, 93, 1. Of course scholars have not failed to note that the hoplites were to be found there and they went to the only edifice large enough to accommodate them. In fact, the same place was sometimes chosen for its proximity and sometimes for its size.

57. Thucydides, VIII, 93, 3; in order to explain this choice, Antony Andrewes and Kenneth James Dover hesitate in their commentary between the idea that a temple could convey solemnity and that the "crowd would have been too large to be accommodated on the Pnyx"; in short, it seems that these places could suit any explanations one might adopt, depending on the number of participants imagined.

58. Thucydides, VIII, 97, 1; note that Thucydides specifies that others *puknai ekklēsiai* were held at the time, assemblies that were "frequent" or "frequented," according to the

"popular" (but all the more current) etymology that connects the name of the Pnyx to *puknos,* meaning tight (Chantraine).

59. Demosthenes, *Against Midias,* 216, *en hieroi d'hoi tauta krinontes kathezomenoi* (concerning the assembly on the subject of the Grand Dionysia, but it is also true of the others).

60. "Dionysus, except by accident or artifice, is a stranger to politics. Not hostile, but serenely indifferent" (Louis Gernet, quoted in Henri Jeanmaire, *Dionysus,* in *Anthropology of Ancient Greece* [Paris: Payot, 1968], 85).

III. Tragedy and the Antipolitical

1. This term was used as the title of an article by Diego Lanza and Mario Vegetti, published in *Quaderni di Storia* (1975): 1–37.

2. See Nicole Loraux, "Reflections of the Greek City on Unity and Division," in A. Molho, K. Raaflaub, and J. Emlen, eds., *City-States in Classical Antiquity and Medieval Italy* (Ann Arbor: University of Michigan Press, 1992).

3. See Nicole Loraux, *La cité divisée. L'oubli dans la mémoire d'Athènes* (Paris: Payot, 1997).

4. Emile Benveniste, "Expression indo-européenne de l'immortalité," *Bulletin de la Société de Linguistique* (1937): 109, 111.

5. Aristotle. *Politics,* III, 1276a, 34–40.

6. Thucydides, I, 2, p. 2 (Archeology); II, 36, p. 107 (Pericles' *epitaphios*). On these elaborations, see Loraux, "Les mots qui voient," in C. Reichler, ed., *L'interprétation des textes* (Paris: Minuit, 1989), and *Born of the Earth: Myth and Politics in Athens,* trans. Selina Stewart (Ithaca: Cornell University Press, 2000).

7. Thucydides, II, 37, 3 (Pericles' *epitaphios*).

8. *Constitution of Athens,* 41, 2. See Loraux, *La cité divisée.*

9. Aristotle, *Politics,* III, 1276a, 15–21.

10. Sophocles, *Ajax,* 645. The reader will notice the biological and natural connotation of *ethrepsen,* obviously conforming to the Sophoclean predilection for this use of the verb *trepho,* but in this case entirely relevant in correlation with *aion.*

11. Aeschylus, *The Persians,* 443.

12. Euripides, *Electra,* 1268–1269, *Hode nomos tethēstai, / nikan, isais psēphoisin ton pheugont' aei* (about the equality of suffrages benefiting the accused according to the formula called "Athena's vote").

13. *Antigone,* 166. Since then, I have considerably altered the analysis of Creon, called tyrant and not king (see Nicole Loraux, ed., Sophocles, *Antigone,* [Paris: Les Belles Lettres, 1997]). Similarly, I would add *Oedipus the King,* 1222, where the messenger greets the chorus as *Oi ges megista tesd' aei timōmenoi* (which underlines the continuity beyond the vicissitudes of the present). The same study could apply to Oedipus, the undefeated—at least he thinks he is. See the work of Anne Dufourmantelle and Jacques Derrida, *Of Hospitality* (Paris: Calmann-Lévy, 1997); Jean Alaux, "Fratricide et lien fraternel. Quelques repères grecs," *Quaderni di Storia* 46 (1997), especially pp. 113–118 (the suicidal eros of Oedipus's sons), and also "Sur quelques pièges de la parenté. Soeurs et frères dans la tragédie athénienne," *Annali della scuola normale superiore di Pisa* 25 (1995): 237–241, and Isabelle Châttelet, "Nommé au malheur," *Césure* (1998) [Apolis]: 125–134, and especially p. 129, "without friends, without [country] city [*apolin*], in solitude"; I have retranslated *polin* as city-state, a term more applicable to ancient Greece.

14. Euripides, *Suppliant Women*, 1172–1173 (*ek teknōn aei teknois / mnemēn paraggellontas*).

15. See especially examples from Euripides; see *Heraclides*, 329, *Suppliant Women*, 341, but also Sophocles, *Ajax*, 599 (eulogy of Salamine).

16. Euripides, *Suppliant Women*, 787; cf. Sophocles, *Oedipus at Colonus*, 1453–1454, *Horai, horai taut' aei / Khronos*, in *Antigone* (184); however, it is Zeus whom Creon credits with seeing all.

17. See Sophocles, *Antigone*, 456–457 (the unwritten laws), *Oedipus at Colonus*, 678–679 (Dionysus); Euripides, *Hippolytus*, 1330 (the divine law); *Ion*, 7 (Phoibus), 1414 (Athena); the time of the cult, for the gods and for the heroes: Sophocles, *Oedipus at Colonus*, 788 (Oedipus); Euripides, *Heraclides*, 777 (Athena), *Hippolytus*, 1426–1427 (Hippolytus), *Helen*, 1699 (Helen). In *Ajax* (1036–1037), Teukros knows that "the gods always contrive misfortunes for men": *Egō men oun kai tauta kai ta pant' aei / phaskoim' an anthrōpoisi mēkhanan theous.*

18. For example, Sophocles' *Antigone*, 1159; Euripides, *Heraclides*, 610.

19. Pierre Vidal-Naquet, *Le chasseur noir* (Paris: Maspéro, 1981).

20. Aeschylus, *Eumenides*, 990–992 (*mega kerdos horo / toisde politais; tasde gar euphronas /euphrones aiei mega timontes*).

21. Sophocles, *Women of Trachis*, 103–104.

22. The malady being that which, in *Philoctetes*, rules the occurrences of *aei*. For example, see 259 and 649.

23. The chorus of *Agamemnon* knows that the only sleep over which *aei* rules is death: *Ag.*, 1448–1451 (*ton aiei . . . / . . . ateleuton hupnon*).

24. Athena, *Ajax*, 1–2, *Aei men, o pai Lartiou, dedorka se / peiran tin' ekhthron harpasai thēromēnon* (wisely, Ulysses uses the adverb *palai*, 20); *Ajax*, 379–380. See also Elisabeth Weber, "La tribu des larmes, prompte à se lever. En marge d'un texte de Jacques Derrida," *Césure* 13 (1998): 219–220 (proper names of Romeo and Juliet in Shakespeare, *Romeo and Juliet*).

25. See the use of *aei* in relation to women in Sophocles' *Electra*, 1239–1242, as well as in Euripides' *Andromache*, 181–182. M. Ierulli defended a thesis on *Electra* in 1998 at Cornell University, which I personally encouraged her to finish quickly.

26. Concerning *Aei* and the Erinyes, see Aeschylus, the *Eumenides*, 76; Sophocles, *Ajax*, 835–837; Euripides, *Iphigenia in Tauris*, 970–971 (concerning the Erinyes remaining faithful to their role as Erinyes).

27. Sophocles, *Electra*, 176, concerning which we may recall Herodotus's use of the verb *uperaxyomai* in VI, 21. See also 222 (*ou lathei m'orga*).

28. See *Electra*, 147–149 (note that if, in 150–152, the reference to the nightingale is made in the style of *aei*, that of Niobe is made in the style of *aiai*). On the nightingale, see Loraux, *La cité divisée*.

29. On this type of statement, see Loraux, *La cité divisée*.

30. *Electra*, 218–219; see also 235 (*mē tiktein s'atan atais*).

31. *Trachiniai*, 28.

32. *Electra*, 852, 1024, 1085.

33. Euripides, *Andromache*, 91–95; *Trojan Women*, 119; *Suppliant Women*, 971–979; *Electra*, 140–147; *Iphigenia in Tauris*, 1089–1095. There would be much to say about the bird as a figure of feminine grief; see Sophocles, *Electra*, 242–243 (the wings of Electra's song), the halcyon of *Iphigenia in Tauris*, the omnipresent nightingale, and, in *Agamemnon*, Cassandra's swan-song.

34. *Constitution of Athens*, 19, 3.

35. From which we have the epithet *prodosetairon* (traitor to his friends) applied by the skolion to the battle of Leipsydrion.

36. It is thanks to Maria Casarès, the incomparable Hecuba of the theater of Gennevilliers in 1988, that I now understand that *aiai* not only should not be translated by "Alas," but ought not to be translated at all. More recently Jean-Max Gaudillière reminded me of the theme of equivalence between *aei* and *aiai,* in his seminar in 1997/98. Finally, and I should have begun with this, *aianes,* which so bothers Chantraine, is caught between lugubrious and always; proof that, even in the absence of a linguistic basis, the Greek ear hears it, as if it were self-evident.

37. *Iliad,* XIX, 301–302 (*Hōs ephato klaious', epi de stenakhonto gunaikes, / Patroklon prophasin, sphon d'auton kēde' hekastē*).

38. Sophocles, *Electra,* 135–150.

39. Sophocles, *Oedipus at Colonus,* 1734–1736: *Aiai, dustalaina, / poi det' authis od' eremos aporos / aiona tlamon' hexō.* Euripides, *Helen,* 211–214.

40. Euripides, *The Phoenician Women,* 330 (*pothon amphidakruton aei katekhōn*) and 335 (*sun alalaisi d'en aiagmatōn*).

41. Aeschylus, *Choephori,* 1017–1020 (1019: *aiai aiai*); Euripides, *Orestes,* 316–321

42. Aeschylus, *The Persians,* 331 (in 332, *kōkumata*), 673 (in 674, *poluklaute*); *Choephori,* 789, 1007, 1009. Euripides, *Alcestis,* 215, 228, 872, 889; *Heracles,* 1025 (stasimon in which Prokne's murder of his son has just been mentioned); *Iphigenia in Tauris,* 146–147, and *Helen,* 165 (in passages that list a surprising accumulation of signs of mourning).

43. Or from the lyrical to the abyss, as in the passages cited above from *Helen* or from *Iphigenia in Tauris,* in which the lyricism takes itself as object, self-referentially.

44. *Trojan Women,* 105 (repeated) 130, 193, 197 (repeated), 238, 241, 579, 628–629 (where we find *aiai mal' authis*), 722, 1226, 1229.

45. Not until 651–653 does Ajax finally acknowledge the truth of his situation.

46. Sophocles, *Ajax,* 370 (*aiai aiai*).

47. *Ajax,* 430–432.

48. See Charles Segal's brief but accurate remarks, in "Song, Ritual and Commemoration in Early Greek Poetry and Tragedy," *Oral Tradition* 4 (1989): 343, on this purely lyrical dimension—metrically speaking—of the final dialogue between Creon and the chorus.

49. *Antigone,* 1267 (seven lines after her first reappearance), 1288, 1290, 1306, 1310. "Unhappy woman . . . ," 1262–1263. For a different perspective, see Loraux, ed., Sophocles, *Antigone.*

50. *Electra,* 1404.

51. Phaedra, *Hippolytus,* 208, 569, 594; Theseus, 806; the chorus, 813, 830, 881; *Hippolytus,* 1070 (1255, the chorus), 1370, 1444. Concerning Racine's *Phèdre,* Serge Koster puts the play first (*Racine. Une passion française* [Paris: PUF, 1998], chap. V, pp. 133–152).

52. *Hecuba,* 182, 229 (Hecuba), 332 (Choryphaeus), 685, 702 (Hecuba); 1022 (Polymestor).

53. N. Loraux, *Mothers in Mourning,* trans. Corinne Pache (Ithaca: Cornell University Press, 1998).

54. *Iliad,* XXIV, 720–722 (Hector's funeral).

55. See also *Ajax,* 994–996 (*aniasasa* in line 994, *Aias* in line 996) and 1005 (*anias*).

56. The text specifically recalls *dusaiane boan,* the "sorrowful cry."

57. *The Persians,* 935–940.

58. *Ie/ia,* see Chapter V.

59. This is not the Attic meaning of this word, tied to the function of the liturgies in the city-state, but the original meaning, in the context of the lyric poem (for further de-

tails, see Gregory Nagy, *Pindar's Homer: The Lyric Possession of an Epic Past* [Baltimore: Johns Hopkins University Press, 1990]).

60. *The Persians,* 1038–1039; see also *diainomai* (1047) and *diainou* (1065), *ani' ania* (1061, 1065), and *aiaktos* (1068).

61. *Poetics,* 1458a 22–23.

62. Or even *lampros,* a way to express "clarity" of discourse by having recourse to the vocabulary of the visual: see Maarit Kaimio, *Characterization of Sound in Early Greek Literature,* Commentationes Humanarum Litterarum 53 (Helsinki, 1977), pp. 47, 224.

63. *The Persians,* 950–951; see 1011 (*Iaōnon*), in response to Xerxes' *hoiai di' aiōnos nikhai* (1008), and the final cry *Ioa* (1070–1071).

IV. The Dilemma of the Self and the Other in Tragedy

1. See Nicole Loraux, *La cité divisée. L'oubli dans la mémoire d'Athènes* (Paris: Payot, 1997).

2. Herodotus, VI, 18–21.

3. The term *pathos* (which in Herodotus also means injury, trauma) is used by Herodotus and Thucydides to designate an evil affecting an entire city.

4. *Pantes hēbēdon,* all citizens of age—in other words the entire civic body, designated by the most official of expressions—had shaved their heads (VI, 21).

5. The verb Herodotus uses is *huperakhthesthentes,* which calls to mind Electra's *huperalge kholon* (Sophocles, *Electra,* 176).

6. Here I am paraphrasing Gregory Nagy, *The Best of the Achaeans: Concepts of the Hero in Archaic Greek Poetry* (Baltimore: Johns Hopkins University Press, 1979), pp. 113–114, on the need for the audience of the cycle to be uninvolved in the death of the hero Achilles.

7. See Jean-Pierre Vernant and Pierre Vidal-Naquet, *Mythe et tragédie en Grèce ancienne II* (Paris: La Découverte, 1986).

8. Sophocles, *Ajax,* 260; *Antigone,* 1187.

9. See above, Chapter II.

10. Examples are found in Aeschines, *Against Ctesiphon,* 153, *hērōikois pathesi.* See also *Panathenaicus,* 168, and in *Panegyricus,* 52ff. Isocrates recalls "tears shed for the evils portrayed on the stage by the poets" (to which he contrasts "real suffering").

11. *Ion* skirts disaster, just missing it, and in the *Eumenides,* the Erinyes become, from powers settled nowhere, benevolent resident divinities (*metoikoi*); in general, in *The Eumenides, Oedipus at Colonus,* Euripides' *Suppliant Women,* or *Heraclides,* Athens acquired an unbreakable alliance with a city-state, or won protection from a hero. However, this did not preclude some residual but fundamental ambiguity *in fine*—as Simon Goldhill analyzes it, in the *Oresteia*— and perhaps in every case.

12. Isocrates, *Panathenaicus,* 121–122.

13. Christian Meier, *De la tragédie grecque comme art politique* (Paris: Les Belles Lettres, 1991), p. 93.

14. Paul Mazon, *Aeschylus,* vol. 1 (Paris: Les Belles Lettres, 1958), p. 59.

15. Ibid.

16. In Lysias, in particular, see *Epitaphios,* 2, *pantakhēi de kai para pasin anthrōpois hoi ta hautōn penthountes kaka tas toutōn aretas humnousi;* see also remarks by N. Loraux, *The Invention of Athens: The Funeral Oration in the Classical City,* trans. Alan Sheridan (Cambridge: Harvard University Press, 1981), p. 337.

17. *Persians,* 286–289; in 284–285, the messenger professes his hatred (*ekhthos*) for the name of Salamis and the groans that the memory of Athens cause him. We notice that

the *stugnai g'Athanai daiois* of the chorus becomes, in Xerxes, more forcefully, *stugnas Athanas* (974).

18. Loraux, *Invention of Athens,* p. 50.

19. Gorgias, fr. DK B 5b.

20. For an example of the identification of Greeks as "other men," see Lysias, *Epitaphios,* 26 and 27; on the gap between *andreia* (Athenian by definition) and the human condition, see Loraux, *Invention of Athens,* p. 337.

21. In the same line (*Frogs,* 1026), the text plays on the two meanings of the verb *didaskein,* "to teach" and "to stage a play," which should please those who read tragedy as strictly political (Peter Euben, for example, in *Greek Tragedy and Political Theory* [Berkeley: University of California Press, 1986], p. 10).

22. *Frogs,* 1055; the poet is the "schoolmaster" (*didaskalos*) of the *hebontes* in particular.

23. See Paul Mazon, "Note on *Perse,*" in Mazon, ed., *Aeschylus,* vol. 1 (Paris: Les Belles Lettres, 1958), p. 56, on the difference between women, "who only mourn those close to them," and the Faithful, "who are capable of assessing the historical importance of the defeat suffered by the Barbarians." In addition, according to Aristophanes himself: (1) tragedy seems to have learned from Phrynichus how to stage despair (*Frogs,* 908–913); (2) Phrynichus's music was sweet, as indicated by the hapax *arkhaia melisidonophrunikhērata* (*Wasps,* 219). Finally, we notice that on several occasions, Aeschylus's tragedy, recalling the grief of the Persian women, reminds us of that of Phrynichus (*Persians,* 133–139; 536–545).

24. More political, in any case, than that of Phrynichus, whose *Phoenician Women,* according to Mazon, "must have been less a tragedy than a cantata" ("Note," p. 56).

25. See, for example, Meier, *De la tragédie grecque comme art politique,* pp. 9–10, and Mario Vegetti, *L'etica degli antici* (Rome-Bari: Laterza, 1989), pp. 49–50, a correspondence all the more interesting because, for the most part, the analyses of these two books disagree.

26. See also Martin West, in his *Studies in Aeschylus* (Stuttgart: Teubner, 1990), on the *Persians,* pp. 75–79.

27. Passages cited: *Persians,* 651, 656, 664, 671, 672 (all designated in 686 as a threnody for Darius); 116, 121, 568–570, 573, 576–578, 581; 1067, 1069, and 1073, 1070–1071, 1075–1076.

28. See remarks by Pietro Pucci, *The Violence of Pity in Euripides' Medea* (Ithaca: Cornell University Press, 1980), p. 28, on the tragic charm (*kerdos*) of tears as a cure for grief.

29. See Meier, *De la tragédie grecque comme art politique,* p. 95, on the difficulty we have in thinking this of the Athenians.

30. See Evanghélos Moutsopoulos, "Sophocle et la philosophie de la musique," *Annales de la Faculté des lettres et sciences humanes d'Aux* 33 (1959), p. 109, on a passage in *Laws* comparing *khara* and *khoros.*

31. See Gregory Nagy's analysis in *The Best of the Achaeans,* pp. 99–100 and 113, on the combinatorial *akhos/ penthos/ kleos* in the reception of the epic.

32. Ibid., 101. As Pietro Pucci points out, the important fact is that now Odysseus is in the position of listener and not of agent (*Odysseus Polutropos* [Ithaca: Cornell University Press, 1986], p. 222.

33. Euripides, *Trojan Women,* 208–209 and 803; and a more neutral evocation in *Hecuba,* 466–474.

34. In addition to Helen's "song without mourning" (*nēpenthēs*) in Book IV of the *Odyssey,* there is Hesiod's *Theogony,* 98–103.

35. See above, Chapter II.

36. See Jean-Pierre Vernant and Pierre Vidal-Naquet, *Mythe et tragédie en Grèce ancienne I* (Paris: Maspéro, 1972).

37. I am using the word here in Gregory Nagy's sense, referred to in both *The Best of the Achaeans* and *Pindar's Homer: The Lyric Possession of an Epic Past* (Baltimore: Johns Hopkins University Press, 1990).

38. From this perspective, comedy, as performed at the Lenaea where, according to Aristophanes, the Athenians were "among themselves," can be more plainly classified as internal. As evidence for the "panhellenic" nature of the Great Dionysia's audience, we recall Isocrates' indignation at the idea of tribute being transmitted in the theater, in front of the allies, and Aeschines' fury at the idea of crowning Demosthenes in front of all the Greeks.

39. *Alien is native:* this notion runs throughout Gregory Nagy's *Pindar's Homer,* especially chapter 10 of that work.

40. *Worship your enemy:* The theme is developed in Margaret Visser's article "Worship Your Enemy: Aspects of the Cult of Heroes in Ancient Greece," *Harvard Theological Review* 75 (1982): 403–428.

41. For example, see Visser's analysis (ibid., pp. 412–415) of Eurystheus in Euripides' *Heraclides.*

42. However, distance is maintained in the word *metoikos,* most of the time, in regard to the Erinyes, in *Oedipus at Colonus* (see Vidal-Naquet, *Mythe et Tragédie II*).

43. Pucci, *The Violence of Pity in Euripides' Medea* (Ithaca: Cornell University Press, 1980), pp. 69 and 170.

44. This means, as interpreters of Aristotelian *katharsis* believe (including Lacan, in his analysis of Antigone), that pity has to be internal to the tragic action.

45. Thucydides, III, 40, 3: *Eleos . . . pros tous homoious.*

46. Loraux, "La métaphore sans métaphore. A propos de l'*Orestie,*" *Revue philosophique* (1990), and *Born of the Earth: Myth and Politics in Athens,* trans. Selina Stewart (Ithaca: Cornell University Press, 2000).

47. *Persians,* 60, 73, 532, 901, 914–915, 920 (the Persians); 234, 349.

48. The chorus is far more nostalgic than the queen and, if only responding to Xerxes, refers to *andres* right up to the end.

49. *Persians,* 94, 99–100: *dolomētin d'apātan theou/ tis anēr thnatos aluxei; / . . . / . . . / . . . broton eis arkuas Ata, / tothen ouk estin huper thnaton/ aluxanta phugein.*

50. *Persians,* 420 (the messenger), 599 (the queen), 632, 706, 710, 749, 820–821 (scene with Darius).

51. On the matter of tragedy as a whole, see Loraux, "Ce que les *Perses* ont peut-être appris aux Athéniens," *Epokhe* 3 (1993).

52. Two occurrences in *Persians,* 432 (losses were counted in *anthrōpoi,* not in *andres*) and 706. On the question of the whole raised by this phenomenon (with the quasi-exception of the use of *anthrōpos* in Sophocles), see my article cited in the previous note.

53. This was pointed out to me by Claude Calame, who attended a lecture in which an early version of this article was presented.

54. Sophocles, *Ajax,* 125–126; See Pucci, *The Violence of Pity in Euripides' Medea,* p. 173, for a reading of this passage from the perspective of Odysseus's pity for Ajax.

55. Hesiod, *Works and Days,* 90.

56. This is no doubt one of the essential definitions of human life in tragedy; the appearance of the Erinyes in *Eumenides* is a striking variant, "suppressing all distinctions between the place of the dead and the place of the living," because the Erinyes "do not try

to kill Orestes, but to drag him, alive, away into the shadow of death" (Diego Lanza, "Les temps de l'émotion tragique," *Mētis* 3 (1988): 21).

57. Athena designates Ajax as an enemy (*ekhthros*) for Odysseus (*Ajax,* 2), but he changes her word to "hostile" (*dusmenēs,* 18); see Mary Whitlock Blundell, *Helping Friends and Harming Enemies* (Cambridge: Cambridge University Press, 1989), p. 63, who remarks on this and observes that Odysseus means that it was Ajax who initiated their enmity.

58. One might have thought that the precept *Helping Friends and Harming Enemies* arose out of a more pointed analysis of the whole than the admittedly psychological reading of M. W. Blundell.

59. Apparently this is a question asked by Athena, but, as Blundell notes (ibid., p. 62), the *oukoun* takes his assent for granted; see W. B. Stanford, *Greek Tragedy and the Emotions: An Introductory Study* (London: Routledge, 1983), pp. 23–26, on the intensity of pity, translated as "compassionate grief."

60. Pucci, *The Violence of Pity in Euripides' Medea,* 173.

V. Song without Lyre

1. At present this question is less an issue in France than in the United States (Helene Foley, Charles Segal), where it is approached from the perspective of neo-Hellenic studies (Gail Holst-Warhaft, *Dangerous Voices: Women's Laments and Greek Literature* [New York: Routledge, 1992]).

2. Even though this prohibition is not explicitly formulated like that concerning the origin of language during the nineteenth century by the Société de Linguistique de Paris.

3. Jean-Pierre Vernant says that the question is a false one: J.-P. Vernant and Pierre Vidal-Naquet, *Myth and Tragedy,* trans. Janet Lloyd (New York: Zone Books, 1990), p. 23.

4. We know what speculations have arisen out of Herodotus's passage on Cleisthenes of Sicyon's authoritative attribution to Dionysus of the cult originally devoted to the hero Adrastus, whose misfortunes (*ta pathea*) were celebrated by "tragic choruses" (Herodotus, V, 67).

5. See N. Loraux, "Les mots qui voient," in Claude Reichle, ed., *L'interprétation des textes* (Paris: Minuit, 1989).

6. Aristotle, *Poetics,* book 4. See the comments of J. Lallot and R. Dupont-Roc on Aristotle's use of the verb "to be a protagonist" (*protagonisteuein*) to characterize the role of *logos* beginning with Aeschylus. Aristotle is thinking in terms of the evolution of the genre toward a *telos;* perhaps because, unlike Aristotle, we do not have the complete range of the genre, we have a tendency to archaize Aeschylus.

7. This view, moreover, seems to be, almost "naturally," given the works available to us, that of historians of the genre; consider Arthur Pickard-Cambridge's comment in *The Dramatic Festivals of Athens* (Oxford: Clarendon Press, 1968), p. 232, in reference to *Agamemnon:* "The chorus comes nearest to dominating the whole."

8. See Charles Segal, "Song, Ritual, and Commemoration in Early Greek Poetry and Tragedy," *Oral Tradition* 4 (1989): 341–342.

9. John Herrington, *Poetry into Drama. Early Tragedy and the Greek Poetic Tradition* (Berkeley: University of California Press, 1985).

10. Gregory Nagy, *Pindar's Homer: The Lyric Possession of an Epic Past* (Baltimore: Johns Hopkins University Press, 1990), 108–109.

11. Ibid., p. 82.

12. Aeschylus, *Choephori*, 423–424. This also recalls for example the fragment from Euripides' *Hypsipyle* (I, 3, v. 9), ". . . the dirge (*elegon*) of Asia, *ieïon* . . . "

13. On Aristotle's emphasis upon this tradition in book VIII of *Politics*, see Gilbert Rouget, *La musique et la transe. Esquisse d'une théorie générale des relations de la musique et de la possession* (Paris: Gallimard, 1990), pp. 397, 400.

14. See above, Chapter IV.

15. Maarit Kaimio, *Characterization of Sound in Early Greek Literature*, Commentationes Humanarum Litterarum 53 (Helsinki, 1977), observes that the reference to music in expressions designating lamentation is characteristic of the tragic style.

16. For example, Helene P. Foley's reading in "The Politics of Tragic Lamentation" is pronouncedly political: in Alan P. Sommerstein, ed., *Tragedy, Comedy and the Polis: Papers from the Greek Drama Conference* (Bari: Levante, 1993), pp. 101–143.

17. Donna Kurtz and John Boardman, *Greek Burial Practices* (Ithaca: Cornell University Press, 1971), p. 202.

18. Nagy, *Pindar's Homer*, p. 403, on lines 1301–1303 of *Frogs*.

19. According to Margaret Alexiou in *The Ritual Lament in Greek Tragedy* (London: Cambridge University Press, 1974), lamentation often included a dance, frequently performed to the sound of the *aulos*. To be sure, this description relies almost exclusively on Euripidean examples.

20. The *epitumbion ainon* "covered with tears" that is recalled in *Agamemnon*, 1548–1550, may or may not be the same thing as the threnody of line 1541; *Choephori* seem to respond in the affirmative in 334–335 (*epitumbios thrēnos*).

21. *Choephori*, 321, *goos euklees*, which seems to be synonymous with the quotations in the preceding note.

22. *Odyssey*, XXIV, 60–62; and see Nagy's remarks in *Pindar's Homer*, pp. 170–172, 174–175.

23. Plutarch, *Solon*, 21, 6. On the funeral oration, see N. Loraux, *The Invention of Athens: The Funeral Oration in the Classical City*, trans. Alan Sheridan (Cambridge: Harvard University Press, 1981), pp. 44–48.

24. Euripides, *Hecuba*, 1035. For a Greek, the eyes are everything.

25. Sophocles, *Ajax*, 652; see also 581–582.

26. In particular Alexiou, *Ritual Lament in Greek Tragedy*, p. 103.

27. Sophocles,*Philoctetes*, 1401 *(halis gar moi tethrenētai gooïs); Electra*, 104 *(ou men dē/ lexō threnōn stugeron te goōn)*, 232, 255, 530 *(pater houtos sos hon thrēneis aei); antigone*, 1210–1211 *(epos/hiēsi dusthrēnēton)*.

28. For example, *Medea*, 1211, 1249; *Andromacha*, 92; *Hecuba*, 212, 295, 433–434; *Phoenicians*, 1434, 1762; *Iphigenia in Tauris*, 490; *Helen*, 604.

29. *Heracles*, 1053. I have borrowed the lovely expression "negated music" from Segal, "Song, Ritual, and Commemoration," p. 344.

30. Since the use of this term in Aeschylus is generally pertinent, we should no doubt give a disjunctive meaning to *ē* in the expression *eipein rhesin ē thrēnon* (*Agamemnon*, 1322); however, we should still point out that this *thrēnon* is spoken.

31. Aeschylus, *The Persians*, 686; *Agamemnon*, 1541 (*tis ho thapsōn nin; tis ho thrēneson*); *Choephori*, 331–335 (*epitumbios thrēnos*).

32. Euripides, *Suppliant Women*, 87–88.

33. This is the word used by Helene Foley, who remarks on it in passing in a note ("The Politics of Tragic Lamentation," n. 25).

34. Aeschylus, *Agamemnon*, 1322, *eipein . . . thrēnon thelo / emon ton autes*.

35. Aeschylus, *Suppliant Maidens*, 116. I should like to point out that the word used here is, as it should be, *goos;*, as noted even in the epic tradition, a *goos* was primarily a song of self-lamentation for women.

36. Aeschylus, fr. 749a, *thrēnei de goon ton aēdoniōn;* cf. Euripides, fr. 773 (vv. 23–26, *melpei d'en dendresi leptan / aēdon harmonian / orthreuomena goois / Itun Itun poluthrēnon*).

37. See *Electra*, 232 (*hode thrēnon*); cf. *Ajax*, 582 and 631–633; see also Euripides, *Hypsipyle*, I, fr. 4, v. 4.

38. Euripides, *Helen*, 165–166, as well as 1107–1112 (ode to the nightingale, *mouseia . . . thrēnois*), and *Hypsipyle* I, fr. 4, vv. 5 sqq.

39. Euripides, *Phoenician Women*, 1302–1303.

40. Segal, "Song, Ritual, and Commemoration," p. 339: "weeping is in itself a kind of song."

41. See Nagy, *Pindar's Homer.*

42. Aeschylus, *Agamemnon*, 1074–1075.

43. The verb *parastateini* used by the chorus in *Ag.* 1078–1079 belongs to the technical language of drama in which it designates the position of one *choreute* in relation to another; the chorus speaks a language that, though appropriate to its station, sounds odd when applied to Apollo.

44. Euripides, *Suppliant Women*, 975–979.

45. Aeschylus, *Seven against Thebes*, 859–860.

46. Echoing this hostility is the strange juxtaposition of the two gods in Euripides' *Orestes*, 1388–1389, *xeston pergamōn Apollōnion / erinun.*

47. Euripides, *Medea*, 421–428; analogous declarations on the relationship of women to the Muses are found in 1085–1089.

48. Plato, *Republic*, III, 398d–e and 399e. On this passage, see Pickard-Cambridge, *The Dramatic Festivals of Athens*, p. 259.

49. Aeschylus, *Agamemnon*, 1164–1167; concerning this passage, notice that in the *Oresteia*, *peplegmai* is the content itself of Agamemnon's cry when he is killed (*Ag.*, 1343, 1345), but it also denotes the blows that the wailing woman inflicts upon herself in leading the mourning (*Choephori*, 30–31), whereas *phoinios*, which denotes murder, also characterizes the bloody gash on the mourner's cheek (*Choephori*, 24–25).

50. Plato, *Republic*, III, 398d.

51. The same idea is expressed in the tragedies: see Euripides, *Alcestis*, 570; *Iphigenia in Tauris*, 1128–1132, and fragment 477, v. 1.

52. Georges Dumézil, *Apollon sonore et autres essais: Vingt-cinq esquisses de mythologie* (Paris: Gallimard, 1982), pp. 31 and 55.

53. Sophocles, *Oedipus the King*, 186. I realize that this verb also has as the grammatical subject *stonoessa te gerus homaulos*, which seems to counter my argument; however, I am betting that the verb *lampei* is implied by the reference to paean, though it becomes an oxymoron in "the sound of lamentation that goes with the flute"!

54. This parodies the title of an argument in the *Nouvelle Revue de Psychanalyse*, "Whenever someone speaks, it is clear as daylight."

55. Aristotle, *Problems*, XIX, 43 (922a); conversely, the sound of the lyre is called *amiktoteroi tei phonei.*

56. The texts insist on the fusion of instrument and song, *homaulos* in *Oedipus the King*, 186, *sun aulois* in a dithyramb of Pindar (s4, v. 18). It should be noted also that to sing with a lyre implies a higher degree of education than participating in a chorus, to the sound of the *aulos* (Nagy, *Pindar's Homer*, p. 110).

57. See Kaimio, *Characterization of Sound in Early Greek Literature*, p. 195, on the hy-

porcheme of Pratinas in which the chorus of satyrs protests against the dominance of the flute. Also the remarks in Richard Seaford's edition of *Cyclops* (Oxford University Press, 1984), p. 15.

58. See Aristotle, *Politics,* VIII. 1341a 21–22, on the orgiastic flute. On Dionysus and *mania,* see Henri Jeanmaire, *Dionysos* (Paris: Payot, 1970), p. 242; see also Gilbert Rouget, *La musique et la transe. Esquisse d'une théorie générale des relations de la musique et de la possession,* 2d ed. (Paris: Gallimard, 1990), pp. 386–393.

59. Euripides, *Helen,* 1351; Aristophanes, *Clouds,* 313. On the word *barus* for the sound of the flute, see Kaimio's comments—at times obscure ones—in *Characterization of Sound in Early Greek Literature,* pp. 153–154, 190, 200–201, 229–230. Martin West notes that "the instrument had quite a penetrating tone, to judge by the ability of a single pair of *auloi* to accompany a choir of up to fifty men" (*Ancient Greek Music* [Oxford: Clarendon, 1992], p. 105).

60. Rouget, *La Musique et la transe,* p. 391.

61. Compare with Aristotle, *Problems,* XIX, 1: "Why do those who are grieving and those who are enjoying themselves alike have the flute played to them?"

62. It is called sweet in *Bacchae,* 127–128; joyous in *Electra,* 879 (a meta-dramatic passage) as well as *Bacchae,* 380 *(meta t'aulou gelasai);* mournful, in *Trojan Women,* 126; phrygian in *Bacchae,* 127–128 and *Iphigenia in Aulis,* 576–577; barbarian in *Iphigenia in Aulis,* 576–577.

63. "Often accompanied to the harsh music of the *aulos,*" Alexiou, *Ritual Lament in Greek Tragedy,* p. 6.

64. On this topic, see Charles Segal, "Song, Ritual, and Commemoration in Early Greek Poetry and Tragedy," *Oral Tradition,* 4 (1989): pp. 330.

65. *Agamemnon,* 988–991, *ton aneu luras homos humnoidei / thrēnon Erinuos / autodidaktos esothen / thumos:* the position of the verb *humnoidei* between *aneu luras* and *thrēnon,* when heard, creates an oxymoron on two accounts. "Lyre-less" (*aphor/miktos*) will actually be the hymn that the chorus of Erinyes will sing in the *orkhēstra* (*Eumenides,* 332–333).

66. *Iphigenia in Tauris,* 144–147; *Helen,* 185–187. Also see *Sophocles,* fr. 849, L.1. Note that the flute is the normal accompaniment and the characteristic sign of elegy.

67. *Phoenician Women,* 1025–1027 (and 1033–1034). See Ana Iriarte, "L'ogresse contre Thèbes," *Mêtis* 2, 1 (1987): 91–108.

68. Sophocles, *Oedipus at Colonus,* 1222–1223.

69. *Trach.,* 643.

70. Sappho, see fr. 44 Page, devoted to a concert of flutes, lyres, and song, and the remarks of Kaimio in *Characterization of Sound in Early Greek Literature,* p. 131; see also Pindar, *Olympia,* III, 8, sqq., *Pythia,* X, 38 (Kaimio, p. 147).

71. From the myth of Hermes' invention of the lyre (*Homeric Hymn to Hermes*). See Laurence Kahn, *Hermes passe* (Paris: Maspéro, 1975).

72. Euripides, *Alcestis,* 445–447 and 430–431; *Helen,* 169–173 (funeral context); *Iphigenia in Tauris,* 1036–1039 (celebration of Hymenaius).

73. *Heracles,* 688; *Ion,* 6, 681–682, 884, 1075; *Electra,* 1190–1192.

74. Aeschylus, *Agamemnon,* 512 *(paionios),* Tetr. 44 A, fr. 701, v. 6 (contrast between the Dionysian dithyramb and Apollo's paean); Sophocles, *Trachiniae,* 211; Euripides, *Alcestis,* 92, 220; *Heracles,* 687–691, 820–821; *Ion,* 125–127, 906 (Apollo singing a paean), *Iphigenia in Aulis,* 1468 (paean for Artemis), fr. 477, v. 1 *(Paian Apollon eulure).*

75. See also Sophocles, *Oedipus the King,* 1096; *Ieie Phoibe. Ie* in a paean: see Pindar, *Peans,* I, 5; II, 35; IV, 31; VI, 121–122.

76. Aeschylus, *Choephori*, 341–342; Euripides, *Iphigenia in Aulis*, 182–185. See also Aeschylus, *The Persians*, 605; *Ag.*, 1248, and Tetr. 28 A, fr. 279a, v. 4.

77. Sophocles, *Oedipus the King*, 5; also 186.

78. See my discussion of the oxymoron in "La métaphore sans métaphore. A propos de *l'Orestie*" in *Revue Philosophique* (1990): 252–253.

79. *Alcestis*, 447, *alurois humnois; The Persians*, 619–620, 625–626 (Darius will speak of threnody); *Choephori*, 475.

80. Aeschylus, *Seven against Thebes*, 867–870; *Ag.*, 990–991; *Eumenides*, 306. See also *Choephori*, 386–388 (hymn for a man killed).

81. *Iphigenia in Tauris*, 179–185; this remarkable passage joins an oxymoron (*tan en threnoisin mousan* / . . . *Haidas humnei*) with an orthodox dissociation (*dikha paianon*); *Bacchae*, 70–71.

82. Aeschylus, *TrGF* (Radt) 161 v. 3, 255 v. 1 (in which Philoctetes speaks). The latter text probably inspired Sophocles, *Trachiniae*, 1208, and Euripides, *Hippolytus*, 1373.

83. Aeschylus, *Seven*, 635, 870; *Ag.*, 645; Euripides, *Tro.*, 126, 578; *Hel.*, 177; Aeschylus, *Cho.*, 151; Euripides, *Alc.*, 424.

84. See the remarks of Richard Seaford on ambiguity in his notes on line 664 of *Cyclops*.

85. See Aeschylus, *Suppliant Maidens*, 112–116 (*ie ie* / *ielemoisin*) and especially *Choephori*, 424 (*ielemistria*, the name of the weeping woman); Euripides, *Suppliant Women*, 281; *Heracles*, 110; *Trojan Women*, 604 and 1304; *Electra*, 1211 (*ieion goon*); *Phoenissae*, 1303–1307; *Orestes*, 1390.

86. Sophocles, *Oedipus the King*, 173.

87. See Henri Jeanmaire on *ololuge* and *iou iou* on the funeral procession of Dionysus in *Dionysos* (Paris: Payot, 1970), pp. 233, 236, and especially 93–94.

88. See *The Persians*, 936, *kakomeletan ian.*

89. Louis Gernet, "You-you, En marge d'Hérodote," in *Les grecs sans miracle* (Paris: La Découverte–Maspéro, 1983), p. 249. See also W. B. Stanford, *Greek Tragedy and the Emotions: An Introductory Study* (London: Routledge, 1983), p. 23.

90. Plutarch, *Theseusi*, 22, 4.

91. Jeanmaire, *Dionysus*, p. 94.

92. L. Gernet, "You-you," p. 254.

93. Jeanmaire, *Dionysus*, p. 93.

94. Pindar, *Paean VI*, 120, *Iē iete;* Euripides, *Suppliant Women*, 281, *oiktron iēlemon oiktron ieisan*, which we will again compare to *Choephori*, 152 (*iete dakru*). On the "connection by popular etymology" see Chantraine, *Dictionnaire étymologique*, s.v. *iēios.*

95. See Gregory Nagy's etymology of Hesiod's name in *The Best of the Achaeans: Concepts of the Hero in Archaic Greek Poetry* (Baltimore: Johns Hopkins University Press, 1979), pp. 296–297. There are some remarkable examples of the use of the verb *[h]iēmi* in *The Persians*, 636–637, 944.

96. In this regard, I am more radical than Charles Segal in his statement on the connection between tragedy and song "including its debt toward forms of mourning" ("Song, Ritual, and Commemoration," p. 330). I would say that, in fact, tragedy does more than merely include mourning: it is wholly dependent upon mourning.

97. Aeschylus, *Agamemnon*, 709–711. See also Euripides, *Trojan Women*, 515–516, *kainon humnon/* . . . *oidan epikedeion.*

98. Euripides, *Helen*, 173–178. See Aeschylus, *Seven against Thebes*, 866–870.

99. Pindar, *Isthmian Odes*, VIII, 57, sqq. On the recurring tendency in Pindar to connect song and instrumental music, see Kaimio, *Characterization of Sound in Early Greek*

Literature, p. 147. I would also point to Pindar's tendency to connect instruments or forms that tragedy presents as incompatible.

VI. Dionysus, Apollo

1. Aeschylus, *Agamemnon*, 637.
2. This is the expression used later in his speech (*Ag.*, 645), and we have no reason to assume that he is already thinking of the Erinyes.
3. *Ag.*, 646–649. More conscious of the rule of the oxymoron in tragedy, the messenger should have known that in speaking of the "paean of the Erinyes" he has already achieved this mixing, or muddling.
4. W. B. Stanford, *Greek Tragedy and the Emotions: An Introductory Study* (London: Routledge, 1983), p. 53 (contrasting Italian opera in its early years with Greek tragedy). In contrast, Henri Jeanmaire says about the dithyramb that from the beginning of the fifth century, "the sound of instruments made it difficult to hear the poem" (*Dionysos* [Paris: Payot, 1970], p. 233).
5. See Chapter V.
6. For an example, see Aeschylus's *Persians*, 571–575, 633 sqq., 935–939, as well as Hecuba's song in *Trojan Women* (146–148: *klaggan molpan*) or that of the chorus in Euripides' *Phoenician Women*, 1301–1303 (*boai barbaroi / iakhan stenaktan / melomenan nekrois dakrusi thrēneso*).
7. Aeschylus, *Agamemnon*, 121, 139, 159 (*eipe*); Sophocles, *Philoctetes*, 218 (*proboai*); Euripides, *Phoenician Women*, 1519–1520 (*ailinon aiagmasin ha/proklaiō*). See also Sophocles, *Ajax*, 627; Euripides, *Helen*, 171–172, and *Orestes*, 1395 sqq.
8. See Aeschylus, *Suppliant Maidens*, 112–115 (*threomena*). Also *Agamemnon*, 1187 (the chorus of Erinyes: *ouk euphōnos, ou gar eu legei*), 1322 (*eipein . . . thrēnon*), and *Choephori*, 151 (*paiana tou thanontos exaudōmenas*). I am not sure, given these examples, that it is enough to say, like James I. Porter ("Patterns of Perception in Aeschylus," in M. Griffith and D. Mastronarde, eds., *Cabinet of the Muses* [Atlanta: Scholars Press, 1990], p. 52, n. 46), that "for Aeschylus, word and song are, in principle, each a metaphor of the other."
9. One thing seems clear to me at least, in the difficult passage of *The Trachiniae* devoted to the rivalry between the *aulos* and the lyre: in lines 642–643, *theias mousas* has much to do with the Muse.
10. Sappho, fr. 150 Campbell.
11. Euripides, *Alcestis*, 445–447.
12. Aeschylus, *Suppliant Maidens*, 694–695, *euphēmon . . . mousan.*
13. Euripides, *Medea*, 195–197, 421, 1085 and 1989.
14. Aeschylus, *Eumenides*, 308; Euripides, *Iphigenia in Tauris*, 183–184 (cf. 144–145); *Hypsipyle*, fr. 4, vv. 6–9; *Phoenician Women*, 1499. See also *Helen*, 66–167, 173–175, 1107–1112.
15. And even more than music, since, in *Choephori* (467–468), even the blow that struck Agamemnon is described as *paramousos.*
16. See Chapter I.
17. *Trojan Women*, 122–123. Notice that since the chorus has not yet entered, Hecuba's song can actually be said to be "without chorus." More remarkable, of course, in Sophocles' *Electra* (1069) are the "offenses without a chorus" (*akhoreuta oneidē*).
18. Euripides, *Medea*, 830–832; Sophocles, *Oedipus at Colonus*, 692.

19. Sophocles, *Antigone*, 1060–1065; *philaulous t'ērethize Mousas*. See also my edition of the play (Paris: Les Belles Lettres, 1997).

20. R. C. Jebb, ad loc., quoting Pausanias, I, 2, 5. Also, in *Oedipus the King,* retranslated as *Oedipe Tyran* by Philippe Lacoue-Labarthe, in Hölderlin, *Sophocles' Oedipus* (1998), we read: "The drunken Bacchus, god of the *evohe,* / Alone with the maenads; let him come / Burning in the light of his blazing torch, / Against him, the god, / Whom the gods dishonored." The situation is the same: the father, Oedipus, replacing the daughter, Antigone.

21. See Chapter III.

22. Euripides, *Heracles,* 685–686. In the following *stasimon,* the chorus again evokes the Muses of the Helicon (791).

23. Or like a tragic chorus, except that Heracles is the protagonist and cannot be seized by Dionysus without risk. *Heracles,* 871 (Lyssa: *khoreusō kai katauleso*); 878–879 (the chorus: *manikaisin Lussas / khoreuthent'enaulois*); 899 (*bakheusei*); 966; and, of course, 1119 (Heracles, bacchant of Hades).

24. *Heracles,* 1025–1027.

25. In this case, crimes by women.

26. Pietro Pucci was the first to call my attention to this passage in *Heracles* at a conference on the theme of the nightingale.

27. See Gregory Nagy's analysis of this point in *The Best of the Achaeans: Concepts of the Hero in Archaic Greek Poetry* (Baltimore: Johns Hopkins University Press, 1979), pp. 305–306. Would the Muses, who were normally benevolent toward the poet whereas Apollo is characterized as ambivalent toward his *therapon,* become ambivalent in tragedy also?

28. I do mean mourning, and not just the comforting representations of the afterlife which, according to Albert Henrichs, "Between Country and City: Cultic Dimensions of Dionysus in Athens and Attica," in *Cabinet of the Muses,* ed. Griffith and Mastronarde, link Dionysus, the dead, and the earth in cultic rituals.

29. Heraclitus, DK, fr. 80; see also 24.

30. Aeschylus, *Agamemnon,* 1119–1120, 1141–1142. Notice that the Hippocratic treatise *On Sacred Disease* associates cries like those of birds with Apollo Nomios.

31. This includes the verb form *(ep)orthiazo,* of which Aeschylus makes a great deal (Maarit Kaimio, *Characterization of Sound in Early Greek Literature,* Commentationes Humanarum Litteraum 53 [Helsinki, 1977], p. 166); see *Persians,* 687 (*psukhagogois orthiazontes goois*), 1050, *Agamemnon,* 1120 (*Erinun . . . / eporthiazein*); Sophocles, *Antigone,* 1206 (*orthion kokumaton*).

32. *Iliad,* XII, 10; see also *The Homeric Hymn to Demeter,* 432 (the cry of the captive Persephone).

33. *Problem,* XIX, 37. Kaimio, *Characterization of Sound,* p. 166, denies the relevance of this reference without clearly explaining the reasons for this rejection (see also p. 230).

34. *Choephori,* 271 (*kaxorthiazōn*), 955 (*epōrthiazein*).

35. Plutarch, *On the Oracles of the Pythia,* 397a; see also *Génération de l'âme* (*Moralia,* 1030a). Would it be out of place to recall that there is a Dionysus *orthos?*

36. Chantraine, quoted by Kaimio, *Characterization of Sound,* p. 47.

37. Sappho, 44 Campbell, 32–33.

38. We notice as well that, for Cassandra, straight Apollonian prophecy (*orthomanteias*) is a *deinos ponos* (*Ag.,* 1215–1216).

39. Sophocles, *Antigone*, 1152; see also fr. 959, 3.

40. Euripides, *Cyclops*, with an introduction and commentary by Richard Seaford (Oxford: Clarendon Press, 1984), 69–70.

41. Aeschylus, *Persians*, 940, *poludakrun iakhan;* Sophocles, *Oedipus the King*, 1218 (*ou iakheōn* according to the manuscripts, and which perhaps cannot legitimately be replaced by *ian kheōn*); Euripides, *Electra*, 143 (*iakhan Ai'da, melos*) and 1150 where, felled by a mortal blow, Agamemnon cried out (*iakhēse*); *Trojan Women*, 515–516 (the song of mourning for Troy); *Helen*, 1486, *iakkhē* of the syrinx; *Phoenician Women*, 1295 (*nekun olomenon akheso*) and 1302 (*iakhan / melomenan nekrois*); *Orestes*, 826, 965, 1465, 1474; *Iphigenia in Aulis*, 1039. In *Heracles*, 884, the serpents of Lyssa are characterized by their *iakhēmata*.

42. Dionysus, Euripides, *The Bacchae*, 149 (Dionysus receives the name Iakkhos), and fr. 586, v. 4. Apollo, *Heracles*, 782–783 (*pannukhis* for Athena); *Ion*, 498–501 (hymns for Pan in the sunless grottoes); *Trojan Women*, 337, *iakkhē* for Hymeneus.

43. Aeschylus, *Seven*, 635, *epexiakkhasas*.

44. Euripides, *Trojan Women*, 1230, *nekron iakkhon*, and 829, (the *iakkhos* of the bird over the young).

45. Sophocles, *Antigone*, 1135; see also 964 (*euion pur*); Euripides, *Bacchae*, 67, 129, 141, 151, 1034. I should mention the recent publication of Euripides, *Bacchae*, ed. Jackie Pigeaud, éd. (Paris: Les Belles Lettres, 1998).

46. *Oedipus the King*, 208–212; *Trachiniae*, 218–220 (Dionysus), 221 (Apollo/Dionysus, *Paian*).

47. See *Lysistrata*, 1281–1283 (*agekhoron Ieion / Nusion*), 1291–1294 (ie paion / . . . / . . . / *Euoi, euoi, euai, euai*).

48. On the Apollo/Dionysus exchange in the cult around the *epiclēsis Paian*, see the remarks of Claude Calame, *Thésée et l'imaginaire athénien* (Lausanne: Payot, 1990), p. 367. It is not impossible that, rather than a play on the word *euaion*, there is an implicit allusion to *euoi* in the invocations to *Paion* (Sophocles, *Philoctetes*, 826–830) or to *Paian* (*Ion*, 125–127, 141–143, where Apollo is concerned).

49. In the prologue to *The Eumenides*, the Pythia insists on the fact that *Bromios ekhei ton khoron* (24), which signifies that "it holds" or "possesses" Delphi; still, without making the distinction between the cult and the myth of Dionysus that Albert Henrichs wants to see ["Between Country and City: Cultic Dimensions of Dionysus in Athens and Attica," in Griffith and Mastronarde, eds., *Cabinet of the Muses*, p. 258], she continues to evoke the "hare's death" that Dionysus reserved for Pentheus.

50. There is no question that we must step outside tragedy and examine the cults in order to understand Dionysus and Apollo (see Detienne, *Dionysus à ciel ouvert*, Paris: Hachette, 1986, and Heinrichs, "Between Country and City: Dionysus in Attica" in *Cabinet of the Muses*, in which he says "the ambivalent Dionysus of tragedy was a Dionysus for special occasions"). Tragedy is the issue here, however, since it was from tragedy that Nietzsche constituted the pairing of Apollo/Dionysus in order to highlight the specificity of the genre.

51. *Tetr.*, 10 B 86, v. 4; does the rest of the line designate it as "bacchic seer"? Or does it aim at a Dionysian seer? For me, the answer is not clear.

52. Sophocles, *Ajax*, 701 (*Nun gar emoi melei khoreusai*), between the Dionysian dances (700) and the invocation to Apollo (702–705). On the effect of the scherzo characterizing the chorus, see Stanford, *Greek Tragedy and the Emotions*, p. 116.

53. Nietzsche, *The Birth of Tragedy*, trans. Walter Kaufmann (New York: Random House, 1967), chap. 6, p. 54.

54. Ibid., chap. 4, p. 47.

55. *Agamemnon*, 975–983 (*mantipolei d'akeleustos amisthos aoida*); 990–997.

56. *Agamemnon,* 1074–1075, 1078–1079.

57. See 1215 (*deinos orthomanteias ponos*); 1256 (the prophetic fire); 1257 (appeal to *Lukios*). Until he shows himself in this way, during his long speech, he is just like a good archer who has hit his target (*Ag.,* 1194). Aeschylus is no doubt banking on the epic metaphor of "winged" words (literally word-arrows), but how could the author and the listeners forget that Apollo is the archer *par excellence*?

58. *Agamemnon,* 1291, 1323.

59. Marcel Detienne's Apollo the murderer. See *Apollo le couteau à la main* (Paris: Gallimard, 1998).

60. *Agamemnon,* 1081 (*apollon emos*). See Euripides, Fr. 781, v. 12–14, "O Sun of beautiful light, how you have ruined me, with that one. Among mortals, you are rightly called Apollo, by those who know the silent names of the gods."

61. *Agamemnon,* 1047.

62. *Agamemnon,* 1050, the comparison with the swallow is traditionally used to suggest barbarous language (cf. Aristophanes), but found next to the comparison with the nightingale, it suggests a repeated allusion to the myth of Procne. In 1063, moreover, the chorus attributes to her the behavior of a recently captured animal.

63. *Agamemnon,* 1051, *agnota phōnen barbaron,* which Clytemnestra contrasts to the persuasion of her *logos,* since, according to Silvia Montiglio, *Silence in the Land of Logos* (Princeton: Prineton University Press, 2000), it is unthinkable that a silence could be anything other than bad speech.

64. *Agamemnon,* 1062.

65. This will be confirmed in actuality in the *Eumenides* when the Pythia pronounces the prologue and is the first to discover the physical presence of the Erinyes.

66. Plato, *Phaedrus* 244 b–c; the text specifies that it was while in the grip of *mania* and not in their right minds (*sophronousai*) that the oracles best exercised their gift.

67. Like Porter ("Patterns of Perception in Aeschylus," p. 52, n. 46), we can say that the chorus sings resistance to the tragic song.

68. *Agamemnon,* 1108, *pos phraso telos.* On *phrazo,* designating sight in speech, cf. Ana Iriarte, "L'ogresse contre Thèbes," *Mêtis* 2, 1 (1987): 91–108.

69. *Agamemnon,* 1114 (the appearance, *ti tode phainetai*); 1120 (the obvious text, *ou me phaidrunei logos*).

70. Cassandra refuses the comparison because it is not relevant (the nightingale escaped death by metamorphosing into a bird, whereas she will die the most violent death), and because what she sees is real and not metaphorical. In fact, unlike the chorus, she uses no comparison in this part of the scene.

71. See S. Crippa, "Glossolalia. Il languaggio di Cassandra," *Studi italiani di linguistica teorica e applicata* 19 (1990): 494–501.

72. This very eloquent expression is from D. Lanza, "Les temps de l'émotion tragique," *Mêtis* 3 (1988): 28.

73. *Agamemnon,* 1180, 1183.

74. As well as in nonlyric verses (Gregory Nagy, *Pindar's Homer: The Lyric Possession of an Epic Past* [Baltimore: Johns Hopkins University Press, 1990], p. 14); interpreting herself in the possession of the god, Cassandra speaks as her interpreters write.

75. *Agamemnon,* 1186, 1188–1189.

76. N. Loraux, "La métaphore sans métaphore. A propos de *l'Orestie,*" *Revue Philosophique* (1990).

77. *Eumenides,* 500. This will also call to mind all the metatheatrical references, to the dance chorus (307), to the lyre-less song (308, 328–333), to the dance step (370–374).

78. See Porter, "Patterns of Perception," p. 43.

79. *Trojan Women*, 255.

80. Bacchante, 171 (*ekbakkeuousan Kasandran*), 341; maenad, 173, 307 (*mainas thoazei deuro Kasandra dromōi*, the last word evoking Poseidon's statement in the prologue, that Apollo left Cassandra to her frenzy [42, *dromadai*]), 349, 415.

81. On Sartre, see Chapter I; see also the Hellenist Shirley Barlowe's edition of *The Trojan Women* (Warminster, Wiltshire, England: Aris and Phillips, 1986), pp. 173–174, 176.

82. *Trojan Women*, 325–337.

83. *Trojan Women*, 408, *Ei me s'Apollōn exebakkheuen phrenas.*

84. *Agamemnon*, 1256, *papai hoion to pur.*

85. As proof, I cite what she says about *Apollōnos logoi / . . . eis em'hērmēneumenoi* (*The Trojan Women*, 428–429).

86. See Desmond Conacher's remarks on this in "The Trojan Women," in E. Segal, ed., *Oxford Readings in Greek Tragedy* (Oxford: Oxford University Press, 1983), p. 336.

87. *Trojan Women*, 359–365, 384–385, 430.

88. The criticism of laughing in the face of misfortunes recalls the question: "if you know you will die, why are you going there?" (*Agamemnon*, 1296–1298); the obscurity of the song is an allusion to Aeschylus's entire scene.

89. *Trojan Women*, 353, 460; *Choephori*, 148.

90. *Trojan Women*, 356–358; *Agamemnon*, 749; *Trojan Women*, 457. This assimilation of Cassandra into an Erinys and her initial appearance as a torch bearer is no doubt the basis for K. H. Lee's comparison of Cassandra with a Fury.

91. *The Trojan Women*, 356.

92. *Agamemnon*, 1160–1161, *nun d'amphi Kōkuton te kakherousious / okhthous eoika thespiōdesein takha.*

93. The name of the river comes from the verb *kōkuo*, "to lament," "to express cries of grief." Note that, in the *Republic*, III, 387 b–c, this name is first on the list of *onomata panta ta deina te kai phobera* that have to be banished because these names cause a shudder in those who hear them (*Kokutous te kai Stugas kai enerous kai alibantas*).

Conclusion: From Citizen to Spectator

1. For example, *oikos* and *polis*, the study of which peaked with a reading inspired by structuralism, but which must now have the appearance of common ground, a *topos*.

2. Heraclitus, D. K. 80; also 24.

3. See Nicole Loraux, *Tragic Ways of Killing a Woman*, trans. Anthony Forster (Cambridge: Harvard University Press, 1987).

4. See above, Chapter VI.

5. See Chapter III.

6. Philippe Lacoue-Labarthe, *Metaphrasis. Le théâtre d'Hölderlin* (Paris: Presses Universitaires de France, 1998), which refers to Hölderlin, *L'Antigone de Sophocle* (Paris: Christian Bourgois, 1978; 1998).

7. Oliver Taplin, *Greek Tragedy in Action* (London: Methuen, 1978).

8. I am obviously referring to John Winkler and Froma Zeitlin, eds., *Nothing to Do with Dionysus? Athenian Drama in Its Social Context* (Princeton: Princeton University Press, 1990).

9. See above, Chapter IV.

10. Well-argued studies have recently appeared on the subject of purgation in Aristotle: see A. Oksenberg-Rorty, ed., *Essays on Aristotle's Poetics* (Princeton: Princeton

University Press, 1992), and E. S. Belfiore, *Tragic Pleasures: Aristotle on Plot and Action* (Princeton: Princeton University Press, 1992).

11. From this standpoint, Diego Lanza, "Les temps de l'émotion tragique," *Mêtis* 3 (1988), is to my mind an essential reference: Lanza, who has published an edition of Aristotle's *Poetics*, knows all the complexity of the text. The fact that I do not agree with the conclusions of his study does not, in my opinion, diminish its importance.

12. Aeschylus, *The Persians*, 686–687.

13. Gorgias, in the *Hymn to Helen;* and Plato, *Phaedra.*

14. The approach here, in terms of Aristotelian *katharsis,* is the opposite of the one that ascribes to characters feelings of fear and pity that Aristotle appears to attribute to the spectator (see Jackie Pigeaud, *La maladie de l'âme* [Paris: Les Belles Lettres, 1981; 1989]).

15. Hence the views expressed in book VIII of *Politics* on *katharsis* in the area of music are as important, if not more so, for our argument as the corresponding discussion in *Poetics.*

16. Plato, *Republic,* III, 401d, *kataduetai eis to entos tes psukhes* (*The Collected Dialogues* [Princeton: Princeton University Press, 1961]). Let us note once again that, in order to remark on the effects of something on the soul, Plato gives it substance.

17. In addition, the exclusion of the words of the *thrēnos* is construed as a repetition of the exclusion of spoken lamentation; *Republic,* III, 398d–e.

18. Aristotle, *Politics,* VIII, 1341a 21–22.

19. See Arthur Pickard-Cambridge, *The Dramatic Festivals of Athens,* 2d ed., rev. John Gould and D. M. Lewis (Oxford: Clarendon Press, 1968), p. 259; W. B. Stanford, *Greek Tragedy and the Emotions: An Introductory Study* (London: Routledge, 1983), pp. 49–50, on the extent of consensus; also Martin West, *Ancient Greek Music* (Oxford: Clarendon Press, 1992), pp. 31–33.

20. *Problems,* XIX, 27 (919ff.) and 29.

21. A contemporary ethnomusicologist, such as Gilbert Rouget, looking at the conditions that prevail during a trance, would perhaps take issue with the legitimacy of this argument; Gilbert Rouget, *La musique et la transe. Esquisse d'une théorie générale des relations de la musique et de la possession,* 2d ed. (Paris: Gallimard, 1990), passim (and especially p. 21, where music is depicted as "the primary means of manipulating a trance, but by socializing it, not by triggering it"; 60, 163–164, 211–215, 398–399).

22. Stanford, *Greek Tragedy and the Emotions,* p. 118 (who in this case is trying to be consistent with Aristotelian categories). That there is a "permanent alteration in the emotional climate" of some of the tragedies is not in doubt; nor is the fact that most of them end in *eleos.* But a similar category may seem a little too broad.

23. Lanza, "Les temps de l'émotion tragique," p. 17.

24. Ibid., p. 38.

25. *Agamemnon,* 1321–1330. There is a striking disparity between *thrēnon . . . emon ton autes* and the comments on *broteia pragmata.* Doubtless the *oiktirō polu* may call to mind the personal implication that is found in any feeling of pity, but the gravity of Cassandra's speech casts doubt on this line of thought.

26. Let us note that both Stanford and Lanza offer *Agamemnon* as the best example of what Stanford calls affective *peripeteia.*

27. Cf. J. Lacan, *Séminaire VII. L'éthique de la psychanalyse* (Paris: Le Seuil, 1986), pp. 290–300.

28. The benevolent in *Antigone,* 801–805; the sarcastic, 834–838 (compared with Antigone's *Oimoi gelomai* in line 839); the severe, 817–822, 853–856, 872–875 (in the last two cases, however, the chorus is moved and like Antigone, it sings).

29. See above, Chapter III.

30. Among numerous similar definitions of memory, let me refer to that of Lacan in *Le séminaire V. Les formations de l'inconscient* (Paris: Le Seuil, 1998).

31. See Aristophanes' parody of this type of monody in *The Thesmophoriazusae.*

32. This is what the messenger calls Jocasta's "passion" in *Oedipus the King,* line 1240.

33. Lanza, "Les temps de l'émotion tragique," pp. 32, 33, 35.

34. Ibid., p. 35.

35. Ernesto De Martino, *Morte e pianto rituale nel mondo antico* (Turin: Einaudi, 1958).

36. I am thinking of the *huperakhthesthentes* by which Herodotus (VI, 21) characterizes the Athenians' suffering at the news of the capture of Miletus and of the *huperalge kholon* for which the chorus in Sophocles' *Electra* blames the heroine.

37. The study by Jean-Pierre Vernant and Pierre Vidal-Naquet on tragedy's ties to the institutions that it invokes, on the contrary, insists, correctly in my view, upon the fundamental difference that the literary genre introduces into social practices.

38. Even if, as Froma Zeitlin astutely notes apropos of the problematic of Aristophanes' *Thesmophoriazusae,* the meaning of the expression "*mimesis* of X" is quite different depending upon whether the emphasis in this phrase is upon *mimesis* or upon X ("Playing the Other: Theater, Theatricality, and the Feminine in Greek Drama," in H. Foley, ed., *Playing the Other: Gender and Sociability in Classical Greek Literature* [Chicago: University of Chicago Press, 1996], pp. 341–374).

39. See N. Loraux, *Mothers in Mourning,* trans. Corinne Pache (Ithaca: Cornell University Press, 1998).

40. Ibid.

41. On pity, see Chapter IV; on fear, see also Thucydides' comments in book VI (the Athenians' panicked fear of tyranny) and book VIII (the *demos,* immobilized by fear, incapable of resisting the Oligarchy's coup d'état).

42. Stanford, *Greek Tragedy and the Emotions,* pp. 1–2.

43. Lanza, "Les temps de l'émotion tragique," p. 38.

44. Lanza, who always uses the term "spectator" in the plural, observes (ibid.) that the implicit ethics and psychology have their foundation in the individual.

45. Diego Lanza, "Lo spettacolo," in M. Vegetti, ed., *Oralità scrittura spettacolo* (Turin, 1983); Simon Goldhill, "The Great Dionysia and Civic Ideology," *Journal of Hellenic Studies* 107 (1987).

46. See Chapter IV.

47. See Chapter IV again.

48. This, under the name of the Dionysiac, was clearly Nietzsche's intuition.

49. Maarit Kaimio, *The Chorus of Greek Drama within the Light of the Person and Number Used,* Commentationes Humanarum Litterarum 46 (Helsinki, 1970).

50. See N. Loraux, "Les mots qui voient," in C. Reichler, ed., *L'interprétation des textes* (Paris: Minuit, 1990).

51. Stanford, *Greek Tragedy and the Emotions,* p. 43, who believes that all three tragedians turn to this device, cites in particular the example of Aeschylus's *Chorephori.*

52. Gordon Kirkwood, *A Study in Sophoclean Drama* (Ithaca: Cornell University Press, 1958), p. 82.

53. *Oedipus the King,* 895.

54. See Arthur Pickard-Cambridge, *Dramatic Festivals of Athens,* p. 251, for a note on the difficulty of determining the exact motions of the chorus throughout these passages.

55. Nietzsche, *The Birth of Tragedy,* trans. Walter Kaufmann (New York: Random House, 1967), p. 37.

56. *Aeriomai.* Compare this with Aeschylus, *Eumenides,* 372 (*mala gar oun halomena*), and Euripides, *Alcestis,* 962 (*Ego kai diaa mousas / kai metarsios eixa*).

57. Jebb, ad. loc., "*turanne* clearly refers to the *aulos,* not to Apollo or Dionysus": see also Kamerbeek, ad. loc., which quotes the scholiast; Charles P. Segal, "Song, Ritual, and Commemoration in Early Greek Poetry and Tragedy," *Oral Tradition* 4 (1989): 342; Stanford, *Greek Tragedy and the Emotions,* 51–52. Hogan, ad. loc., by contrast, believes that the reference is to Dionysus.

58. In Sophocles' work, this is determining.

59. See Kirkwood, *A Study in Sophoclean Drama,* p. 199. Let us recall that, in Homeric epic, *enarges* denotes the corporeal presence of the god.

60. *Ajax,* 700–701.

61. I have borrowed the expression from Lanza, "Les temps de l'émotion tragique," p. 30, speaking of the hero and not of the chorus; this expression summarizes a number of others in a generic way.

62. The note in the Belles Lettres edition, ad. loc., is awkward, to say the least.

63. On the tragic irony of the work found in this *stasimon,* I suggest the reader see Th. C. W. Oudemans and A. P. M. H. Lardinois, *Tragic Ambiguity: Anthropology, Philosophy and Sophocles' Antigone* (Leyden: Brill, 1987), p. 159; also see N. Loraux, *La cité divisée. L'oubli dans la mémoire d'Athènes* (Paris: Payot, 1997).

64. *Antigone,* 1112. Similarly, in *Ajax,* 706, the chorus of sailors believes that Ares had freed them from suffering forever (*Elusen ainon akhos ap'ommatōn Arēs*).

65. *Antigone,* 1135–1136, *Thēbaias / episkopount' aguias.* This recalls Cassandra's invocation of Aguiates (*Agamemnon,* 1082).

66. See Albert Henrichs, "Between Country and City: Cultic Dimensions of Dionysus in Athens and Attica," in M. Griffith and D. Mastronarde, eds., *Cabinet of the Muses* (Atlanta: Scholars Press, 1990), pp. 265–266.

67. Here Rouget's expression citing Louis Dumont corresponds exactly to the construction in line 1152 (*khoreuousi ton tamian Iakkhon*), which I have attempted to render by my translation.

68. Henrichs, "Between Country and City," pp. 266–269.

69. Unlike Henrichs, I do not believe that we have to see in Antigone an initiate's belief in eternal life. The desire she expresses to be reunited with her family in death does not seem to me to arise from any eschatological hope.

70. ". . . the Chorus . . . , a character or, to be more exact, a group of undifferentiated characters of a drama" (G. Kirkwood, *A Study in Sophoclean Drama,* p. 185, and also p. 186).

71. *Antigone,* 1147, *khorag' astrōn.*

72. *Antigone,* 1149, *prophanēth'.*

73. Henrichs's criticism of a similar analysis ("Between Country and City," p. 266) seems to me irrelevant.

74. *Antigone,* 1144.

75. Henrichs, "Between Country and City," pp. 265, 275, n. 37.

76. Thus, in *ton prokeimenon ti khrē prassein,* I hear a double meaning (*Antigone,* 1334–1335).

ACKNOWLEDGMENTS

In 1993 I was invited by Pietro Pucci to deliver a series of seven lectures at Cornell University on the theme of "The Voice of Song in Tragedy." I was also invited by Gregory Nagy to deliver a lecture at Harvard University on *aei* and *aiai*. I wish now to express to each of them my affection and gratitude.

Laura Slatkin, extending infinite kindness during my visit to New York in 1985, was the first to persuade me to approach the theme of the mourning voice. I want to express my deep appreciation to her as well.

I also wish to thank Molly Ierulli, who translated my lectures at Cornell into American English.

The reading of a wide range of books has influenced my thinking; I wish to mention in particular Victor Hugo's novel of novels, *Les Misérables* (1862), which Jean Maurel encouraged me to reread. The book provided a source of encouragement and hope, which will explain why the reader finds lines from Hugo at the beginning of my book.

I also read the work of Françoise Proust, *De la résistance* (Paris: Le Cerf, 1997); Hölderlin, *Oedipe Tyrannus* (and not *the King*); Honoré de Balzac, *Sarrasine* (1830); and especially, *The Birth of Tragedy* by Friedrich Nietzsche (1869–1872), in the very beautiful translation of Philippe Lacoue-Labarthe (Paris: Gallimard, 1977). This work is quite frankly an improvement over that of Ulrich von Wilamowitz-Möllendorf (*Aischylos Interpretationen* [Berlin, 1914]), who had certainly read everything, but overdid it, in my opinion. And finally, I was inspired by Serge Koster's beautiful work *Racine: Une passion française* (Paris: Presses Universitaires de France, 1998).

Hélène Monsacré undertook the transliteration of the Greek and helped specify a number of citations. I extend my warmest thanks to her.

Finally, from the bottom of my heart, I thank my editor, Eric Vigne.

N. L.

INDEX